Monongahela 1754–55

Washington's defeat, Braddock's disaster

Campaign • 140

Monongahela 1754–55

Washington's defeat, Braddock's disaster

René Chartrand • Illustrated by Stephen Walsh

Series editor Lee Johnson • *Consultant editor* David G Chandler

First published in Great Britain in 2004 by Osprey Publishing,
Midland House, West Way, Botley, Oxford OX2 0PH, UK
44-02 23rd St, Suite 219, Long Island City, NY 11101, USA
E-mail: info@ospreypublishing.com

Transferred to digital print on demand 2010

First published 2004
5th impression 2008

Printed and bound by Cadmus Communications, USA

A CIP catalog record for this book is available from the British Library

ISBN: 978 1 84176 683 6

Editor: Lee Johnson
Design: The Black Spot
Index by Alan Thatcher
Maps by The Map Studio
3D bird's-eye views by John Plumer
Battlescene artwork by Stephen Walsh
Originated by Grasmere Digital Imaging, Leeds, UK

Acknowledgments
J. Martin West at Fort Ligonier, Fort Necessity National Battlefield, the National Archives of Canada (Ottawa), the Public Records
Office (Kew), the Library of the University of Ottawa, and the Library of the Department of Canadian Heritage (Ottawa) were most
kind in providing efficient and timely assistance.

Artist's Note
Readers may care to note that the original paintings from which the color plates in this book were prepared are available for
private sale. All reproduction copyright whatsoever is retained by the Publishers. All enquiries should be addressed to:

info@stephenwalshillustrations.co.uk

The Publishers regret that they can enter into no correspondence upon this matter.

FOR A CATALOG OF ALL BOOKS PUBLISHED BY
OSPREY MILITARY AND AVIATION PLEASE CONTACT:

Osprey Direct, c/o Random House Distribution Center,
400 Hahn Road, Westminster, MD 21157
Email: uscustomerservice@ospreypublishing.com

Osprey Direct, The Book Service Ltd, Distribution Centre,
Colchester Road, Frating Green, Colchester,
Essex, CO7 7DW
E-mail: customerservice@ospreypublishing.com

www.ospreypublishing.com

KEY TO MILITARY SYMBOLS

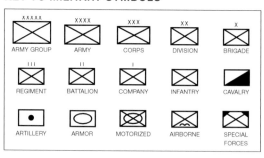

CONTENTS

INTRODUCTION 6
Origins of the campaign

CHRONOLOGY 13

OPPOSING COMMANDERS 14
French • Indian • British • American

OPPOSING ARMIES 18
The French • The Indians • The British and Americans

OPPOSING PLANS 24

FROM JUMONVILLE GLEN 26
TO THE MONONGAHELA
Fort Necessity • The storm clouds gather • Braddock moves west • The battle

AFTERMATH 85

ORDERS OF BATTLE 89

THE BATTLEFIELDS TODAY 91

BIBLIOGRAPHICAL SOURCES 94

INDEX 95

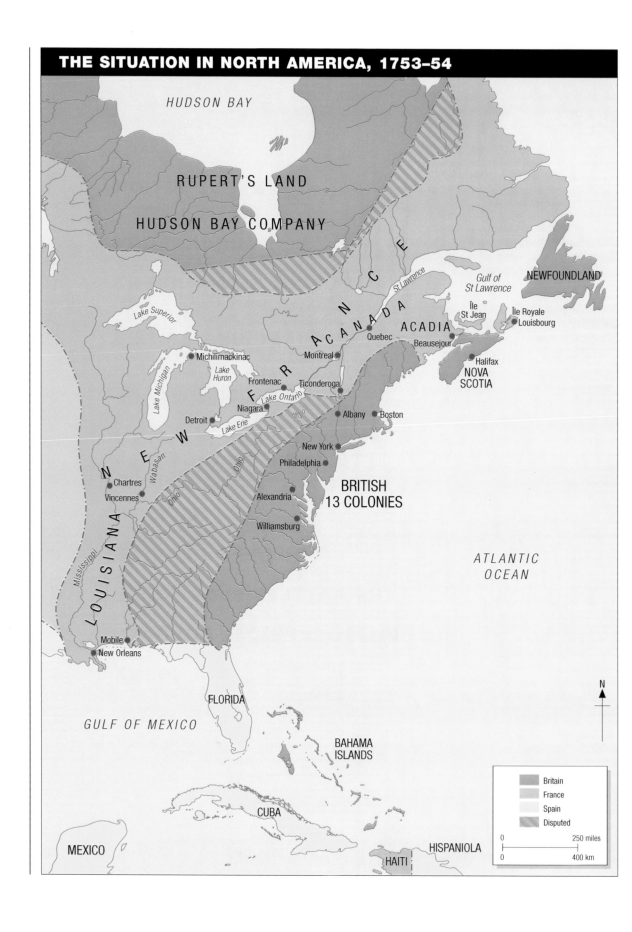

THE SITUATION IN NORTH AMERICA, 1753–54

HUDSON BAY

RUPERT'S LAND

HUDSON BAY COMPANY

NEWFOUNDLAND

Gulf of
St Lawrence

F R A N C E

C A N A D A

St Lawrence

Île
St Jean

Île Royale
Louisbourg

Lake Superior

ACADIA

Quebec

Beausejour

Michilimackinac

Lake
Huron

Montreal

Halifax

NOVA
SCOTIA

Frontenac

Ticonderoga

Lake Michigan

Niagara

Lake Ontario

Detroit

Lake Erie

Albany

Boston

N E W

F R

Wabash

Ohio

New York

Philadelphia

Chartres

Vincennes

Alexandria

BRITISH
13 COLONIES

L O U I S I A N A

Williamsburg

Ohio

Mississippi

ATLANTIC
OCEAN

Mobile

New Orleans

FLORIDA

N

GULF OF MEXICO

BAHAMA
ISLANDS

MEXICO

CUBA

HISPANIOLA

HAITI

	Britain
	France
	Spain
	Disputed

0   250 miles

0   400 km

INTRODUCTION

King Louis XV of France. In the middle of the 18th century, the realm of this somewhat debonair king included parts of southern India and much of North America. This empire, created largely through the efforts of his grandfather Louis XIV, would be lost within the next two decades. Portrait made in 1746 by Maurice-Quentin de La Tour. (Author's photo)

The events related in this book led to a general war, since known as the Seven Years War, between France and Great Britain with their respective allies, that was eventually fought on four continents and culminated in Britain's triumph. The early events at Jumonville Glen, Fort Necessity and at the disastrous field near the Monongahela River have since been overshadowed by the war's subsequent course and by the career of George Washington, destined to become one of the most famous men in modern history.

As will be seen, these early battles ended in utter defeat for the Anglo-American troops at the hand of the "French and Indians", generally seen since as barbarous enemies by generations of American and British historians. However, a closer examination of the "French" show most of them to have been native-born Canadians, and the "Indians" to have been independent peoples won over by their long-standing diplomatic ties with New France. Furthermore, it becomes clear that the "French and Indian" method of fighting was no lucky accident but a conscious tactical doctrine which, ironically, was ignored in France while, after the disaster at the Monongahela, it was eagerly adopted by both British and Americans.

ORIGINS OF THE CAMPAIGN

During the 17th and the first half of the 18th centuries, the British and French colonies in North America, by the very nature of their respective development as well as the frequent wars of their mother countries, were once again moving towards a major confrontation. The British flag flew over a number of colonies stretching from Georgia to Newfoundland along the Atlantic seaboard that were, for the most part, rapidly growing and populous entities. By the middle of the 18th century, the population of the American colonies included well over 1,000,000 souls of European descent. The larger colonies such as Massachusetts, Connecticut, New York, Pennsylvania, Virginia and South Carolina had their own local legislatures, large populations and prosperous economies thanks to the continuing development of agriculture, shipping, trade, and commerce. In spite of some efforts by the Crown to rationalize administration with royal governors, the American colonies remained very independent. They were also quite different from one area to another. The northern colonies, such as Massachusetts, had been settled by religious refugees who often held a "Puritan" and religiously conservative outlook on many of life's issues. The colonists of the middle colonies had more varied origins and New York, for instance, still had a sizeable Dutch population and corresponding traditions. Pennsylvania, although a major trade center thanks to the city of Philadelphia, was still politically dominated by the pacifist sect known as

the Quakers. Of the southern colonies, Virginia was the most important and depended largely on the expanding plantations that gave its society a more distinctive class structure with the large estates and more genteel way of life of its social elite. The government of the British colonies in North America was very decentralized, with each having its own legislative assembly and policies. For all these reasons, in time of war it was difficult to mobilize the colonies into a concerted effort.

New France, by contrast, penetrated deep into the hinterland of North America thanks to outstanding explorers such as Samuel de Champlain who went to the Great Lakes in the early 17th century, Robert Cavelier La Salle who reached the Gulf of Mexico during 1682 by navigating the Mississippi River, and a captain of colonial troops, de La Vérendrye, and his sons who built trading forts in the Canadian prairies and penetrated as far as the Rocky Mountains in present-day Wyoming in the 1730s and 1740s. Except for Cape Breton Island and its fortress and naval base of Louisbourg, built from 1720, France had few coastal settlements until one reached Mobile and New Orleans on the Gulf of Mexico. New France had developed in the interior of the vast North American continent, happy to leave the British colonists to the eastern seaboard and a few posts on Hudson Bay, and the Spanish to Florida and northern New Spain (the present Texas and American Southwest).

There was no gold or silver found in New France and its economic mainstay was the fur trade. To facilitate this trade and maintain its territorial claims, a far-reaching network of forts was built at strategic sites along the shores of the hinterland's rivers and lakes. This network formed a great arc running from the Gulf of the St Lawrence River through the Great Lakes to the Gulf of Mexico. The European population of New France was minuscule and concentrated at either end of this arc: Canada in the north with its approximately 60,000 inhabitants concentrated along the shores of the St Lawrence River; Louisiana with only 5,000 or 6,000 settlers on the Gulf coast and another 2,000 or so established in the "Illinois Country", also called Upper Louisiana, in the area where the Missouri and Ohio rivers

Fur traders and Indians. The fur trade was at the root of the rivalry that led Britain and France to war. In the middle of the 18th century, the French largely controlled the interior of North America and its fur trade, but mounting pressures caused by increasing numbers of Anglo-American traders wandering into the Ohio Valley led to confrontation. Detail for a "map of the inhabited part of Canada from the French Surveys" by C.J. Gaulthier published in 1777. (National Archives of Canada, C7300)

The Marquis de La Galissonière, governor general of New France, 1747–49. He understood the threat to New France should its Ohio communications route be cut by increasing Anglo-American intrusions.

flowed into the Mississippi. Several thousand African slaves had also been transported into Louisiana. As for the indigenous Indian population, it is practically impossible to calculate an accurate figure; many eastern nations had been decimated by epidemics of "European" diseases in the 17th century but sizeable populations remained, while many western nations were all but unknown to Europeans. The government of New France and its components was autocratic, as was France under the "Old Regime". There were no legislative assemblies. The governor general had overall authority, as did the intendant, in financial and civic matters and the bishop in religious issues, with powers devolved to local governors, commissaries and senior priests. In spite of a seemingly rigid autocratic structure, it was necessary to exercise power wisely as all actions had to be approved by senior officials in France who had channels of information and news over and above official reports. One of the benefits of the centralized system of governance in New France was that it was comparatively efficient at mobilizing the colony's relatively meager resources for military purposes.

Communication between Canada and Louisiana was usually along a route west to lakes Erie and Michigan and down the Mississippi via smaller rivers such as the Maumee, Wabash and Illinois. This route was guarded by a string of forts along the shores of the lakes and rivers. The route along the Allegheny and Ohio rivers was known but seldom used other than by occasional roaming traders. During the 1730s and '40s, as the importance of communications between Canada and Upper Louisiana (or Illinois) increased, the vital geostrategic position of the Ohio River became apparent to the French. Considered of negligible economic or political significance and rather wild, with a collection of Indian nations reputedly hostile to strangers, the route was not yet considered worth protecting with forts.

This attitude began to change from the mid-1740s as increasingly frequent reports of Anglo-American traders roaming into the Ohio Valley reached the Château Saint-Louis, residence of the governor general of New France in Québec. Governor General de La Galissonière, one of the French Navy's best admirals, was alarmed at this news. With a perceptive strategic eye, he appreciated the negative impact of allowing gradual Anglo-American penetration of the interior to sever communications via the Ohio Valley. Some of the Indian nations in this hitherto French-influenced area might be convinced to switch their trade and diplomatic allegiances to the Anglo-Americans. The consequences for France would be dramatic and multi-faceted: loss of trade and loss of influence, increasing British activity along the shores of the western Great Lakes, which would in turn drive a wedge into the great arc of French possessions in North America. The dispatches from Québec to Versailles spoke of a looming disaster about to befall New France. However, with the War of the Austrian Succession absorbing the attention of most European powers, including France and Britain, there were other priorities.

With a war raging in Europe, the problem of the Ohio Valley could not simply be dealt with by building a string of forts. New France's limited resources were currently focused on expeditions on the frontiers of New York, Massachusetts and New Hampshire. The French had so far built only one post near the Ohio, Fort Vincennes, and even this was much further west, built in 1731 on the shores of the Wabash River about

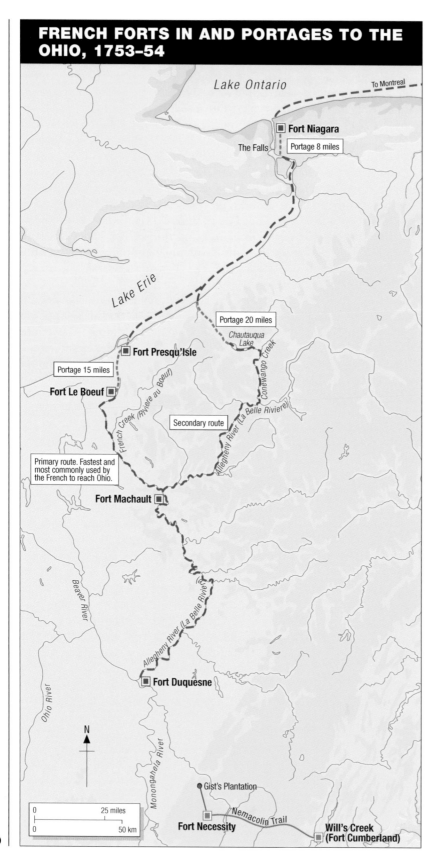

FRENCH FORTS IN AND PORTAGES TO THE OHIO, 1753–54

Lake Ontario

To Montreal

■ Fort Niagara

The Falls   Portage 8 miles

Lake Erie

Portage 20 miles

Chautauqua Lake

■ Fort Presqu'Isle

Portage 15 miles

Conewango Creek

French Creek (Rivière au Boeuf)

Fort Le Boeuf ■

Secondary route

Allegheny River (La Belle Rivière)

Primary route. Fastest and most commonly used by the French to reach Ohio.

Fort Machault ■

Beaver River

Allegheny River (La Belle Rivière)

■ Fort Duquesne

Ohio River

N

Monongahela River

● Gist's Plantation

0   25 miles
0   50 km

■ Fort Necessity

Nemacolin Trail

■ Will's Creek (Fort Cumberland)

King George II of Great Britain, c.1750. As a king, he relied on the advise of his ministers, such as William Pitt, and his reign was a landmark in the development of constitutional monarchy. The king's support of his minister's policies eventually saw outstanding victories across the globe and confirmed Britain as a major world power. Painting by David Morrier. (Fort Ligonier Museum, Ligonier, Pennsylvania. Author's photo)

50 miles north of the meeting of the Wabash and Ohio rivers. Physical occupation of the territory would be the deciding factor, however, and as soon as the war ended in 1748, attention turned to the Ohio. To buy time and make it known to interlopers that the territory was French, an expedition of some 30 soldiers and 180 militiamen with a few Indians left Montréal for the Ohio led by Captain Céléron de Blainville in June 1749. For the next few months Céléron's party roamed the Allegheny and Ohio valleys burying lead plates along the shores of the rivers, effectively claiming the territory for France. Although this was proof positive that the French had indeed occupied the territory, the Anglo-American traders who had formed the Ohio Company in 1748 were not impressed. By December 1749, Céléron was back in Montréal with this alarming news. The Marquis de La Jonquière had by now replaced Governor General de la Galissonière, however. The new governor general was an indecisive man and did not share his predecessor's concerns at the urgency of the situation and the vulnerability of the Ohio Valley. As a result, nothing was done for the next several years as Anglo-American traders penetrated deeper into traditional zones of French influence. They found an ally in Chief Memeska of the Miami Indians, who even raised the British flag in his town of Pickawillany (now Piqua, Ohio). At Fort Michilimackinac, further north, young officer-cadet Charles-Michel Mouet de Langlade, son of a leading fur trader and an Ottawa Indian princess, took matters into his own hands and, without waiting for any approval from Québec or Versailles, led a punitive raid with about 250 Ottawa Indians and a few Canadian militiamen on Pickawillany. On 21 June 1752 the town was surprised and razed to the ground, Memeska killed and eaten by his Indian enemies and the Anglo-American traders captured and sent to Montréal. This was a clear signal to the other Indian nations to value their alliances with the French and they certainly did not miss its meaning.

In Québec, Governor General La Jonquière had passed away in March 1752 and the interim governor general, the Baron de Longueuil, was a veteran and experienced Canadian frontier officer who, like de la Galissonière, felt the Ohio must be occupied urgently. The Marquis de Duquesne, the new governor general, arrived in Canada in August 1752 with instructions from the royal court at Versailles to secure the Ohio Valley. It was clear that the only way to do it efficiently was to build a string of forts to counter the Anglo-Americans. In the spring of 1753, a large force of some 300 soldiers, 1,200 militiamen and 200 Indians left Montréal for the Ohio. Forts Presqu'Isle (Erie, Pennsylvania), Le Bœuf (Waterford, Pennsylvania), also called "de la Rivière aux Bœuf" (now French Creek), and Machault (also called Venango, now Franklin, Pennsylvania) were built during the summer and fall.

In Virginia, Governor Robert Dinwiddie was not about to let the French derail Britain's claims to the Ohio Valley. This area was of great interest to Virginians and had been granted to the Ohio Company formed by Virginian and London businessmen for future settlement and exploitation. Some forays were already being made by frontier trader Christopher Gist to bring in settlers and the young surveyor George Washington. It was also considered to be an area subordinate to the Iroquois Six Nations, allies of the British, and there were some Iroquois there under Chief Tanaghrisson, better known as the "Half-King". Thus to Governor Dinwiddie and those around him, the justification of the Anglo-American claim was quite clear. The French were clearly seizing British territory. If nothing were done about it, their forts would, by actual occupation, legitimize their own claims and the area would be lost to Britain and, more particularly, to Virginia.

The first step was to make it clear to the French that they were intruders; Dinwiddie found that young Major Washington, although inexperienced, was bright and keen to deliver the ultimatum. Accompanied by Gist and a few men, including his translator Jacob van Braam, and the Seneca Indian chief the Half-King, Washington made the long journey into the wilderness to Fort Le Bœuf. On 11 December 1753, Washington delivered Governor Dinwiddie's letters to Commandant Le Gardeur de Saint-Pierre, "a Knight of the Military Order of St Louis" whom Washington described as an "elderly Gentleman, and has much the Air of a Soldier". Washington started back with Gist for Williamsburg to report to Dinwiddie, while de Saint-Pierre had the translated ultimatum sent to Québec. The ultimatum was a signal to both sides to occupy the area as fast as possible. In the spring of 1754, Washington, newly promoted to lieutenant-colonel, was leading 132 Virginia provincial soldiers towards the fork of the Allegheny, Monongahela and Ohio rivers. Washington stopped at Great Meadows with most of his men but a detachment reached the spot which would become the city of Pittsburgh and started building a fort. A few days later, on 16 April, a large force of French and Canadians, under the command of Claude Pécaudy de Contrecoeur, arrived at that strategic spot and ordered the Virginians to withdraw immediately. Heavily outnumbered, the Virginians had little choice but to comply. Contrecoeur's men then continued the construction of the fort, which they named Fort Duquesne. The stage was now set for a confrontation.

CHRONOLOGY

1660s According to French claims, Robert Cavelier La Salle explored the Allegheny and Ohio rivers.

1748 Foundation of the Ohio Company by Virginian traders.

1749 To ensure France's claim, an expedition buries lead plates at various points in the Ohio and Allegheny valleys.

21 June 1752 Punitive expedition against Miami Indians at Pickawillany by French-allied Indians led by Cadet Charles-Michel Mouet de Langlade.

1753 Forts Presqu'Isle, Le Bœuf and Machault built by the French.

12 December Virginia Militia Major George Washington delivers Governor Dinwiddie's ultimatum to evacuate the area to Captain de Contrecoeur at Fort Le Bœuf.

1754

6–7 March The French reconnoiter the forks of the Ohio.

16 April The French arrive in force at the forks of the Monongahela and Ohio rivers (now Pittsburgh, PA) and expel the Virginians who have started to build a fort there. The French complete the fort, which they name Fort Duquesne.

23 May Washington and his Virginians ambush Jumonville's party. Jumonville and many of his men are killed.

26–28 June Captain Coulon de Villiers, Jumonville's brother, arrives at Fort Duquesne with reinforcements and supplies. He vows revenge and takes command of the force sent against Washington two days later.

3–4 July Coulon de Villiers with his strong French and Indian warband surrounds and attacks Fort Necessity, held by Washington and his troops. Washington surrenders and is allowed to return to Virginia the next day after signing a controversial capitulation.

1755

January Two regiments of British line infantry with artillery leave Ireland for Virginia under Major-General Edward Braddock. They land in March.

Spring French troops and Canadian militiamen leave Montréal for the Ohio under de Beaujeu.

3 May French fleet with six battalions of line infantry leaves Brest for New France.

19 June With most ships escaping Admiral Boscawen's attempt to intercept them, four battalions land at Québec, the two others at Louisbourg.

29 May Anglo-American army leaves Fort Cumberland.

18 June General Braddock leaves the slower moving wagons with Colonel Dunbar and presses ahead with about 1,200 of the best troops.

24 June French and Indian raids on General Braddock's column become frequent.

4 July Skirmish in which the French-allied Huron Indians defeat a small party of British-allied Indians.

7 July Anglo-American army reported only nine miles (14.5 kms) from Fort Duquesne. Commandant de Contrecoeur orders a strong party under the command of Captain de Beaujeu to ambush them.

8 July French officers have a grand council to convince the more neutral Indians to join them in attacking the British troops; most do.

9 July Battle of the Monongahela. General Braddock's army is crushed by the French and Indians. Captain de Beaujeu, killed at the beginning of the battle, is succeeded by Captain Dumas.

12 July France's Huron allies leave Fort Duquesne area for Detroit. Many others leave during the following days.

13 July General Braddock dies near Jumonville Glen of the wounds suffered in battle five days earlier.

17 July Remnants of the Anglo-American army reach Fort Cumberland.

8 August Governor General Vaudreuil recalls de Contrecoeur and passes French command in the Ohio to Dumas.

L'AN 1749 DV REGNE DE LOVIS XV ROY DE
FRANCE NOVS CELORON COMMANDANT D'VN
DETACHEMENT ENVOIÉ PAR MONSIEVR LE M.IS
DE LA GALISSONIERE COMMANDANT GENERAL DE
LA NOUVELLE FRANCE POVR RETABLIR LA
TRANQVILLITÉ DANS QVELQVES VILLAGES SAUVAGES
DE CES CANTONS AVONS ENTERRÉ CETTE PLAQVE
AU CONFLUENT DE LOHIO ET DETCHADAKOIN CE 29 IVILLET
PRES DE LA RIVIERE OYO AUTREMENT BELLE
RIVIERE POVR MONUMENT DU RENOUVELLEMENT DE
POSSESSION QUE NOVS AVONS PRIS DE LA DITTE
RIVIERE OYO ET DE TOVTES CELLES QVI Y
TOMBENT ET DE TOVTES LES TERRES DES DEVX
CÔTES JVSQVE AVX SOVRCES DES DITTES RIVIERES
AINSI QVEN ONT JOVY OV DV JOVIR LES
PRECEDENTS ROIS DE FRANCE ET QVILS SY
SONT MAINTENVS PAR LES ARMES ET PAR LES
TRAITTES SPECIALEMENT PAR CEVX DE RISWICK
D'VTRECHT ET D'AIX LA CHAPELLE

Facsimile of the inscription on one of the lead plates buried by Céléron de Blainville's 1749 expedition in the Ohio Valley. This one was buried on 29 July at the fork of the Allegheny and Conewango rivers.

OPPOSING COMMANDERS

FRENCH

There was no single senior French military commander with authority over all others in the French camp. Different officers had command of a variety of forces in the various incidents; indeed two were killed in action. **Ensign Joseph Coulon de Villiers, Sieur de Jumonville**, was the young Canadian officer who led the party into the ambush that would, in time, ignite war between France and Britain. **Captain Louis Coulon de Villiers**, Jumonville's elder brother, was an experienced frontier officer serving in Illinois at the time of the Jumonville Glen ambush. His response upon hearing of his brother's death forms part of the story of this campaign and is related below. The following year he led raids on the Pennsylvania frontier and, in 1756, was at the capture of Oswego and of Fort William Henry. He succumbed to an illness in November 1757.

At the battle of Monongahela, the mixed French and Indian force marching from Fort Duquesne was under Captain Daniel Lienhart de Beaujeu with Captain Jean-Daniel Dumas and Captain François Le Marchand de Ligneris as second and third in command respectively. **Captain Daniel Lienhart de Beaujeu** was the more experienced in frontier warfare and, perhaps most importantly, a talented leader of the Indian nations who respected him as a war chief. His excellent understanding of Indian diplomacy would prove crucial to the battle fought on 9 July. **Captain Jean-Daniel Dumas** was not a Canadian-born officer. He had joined the army at 14 years of age and served many years in the Agenois Regiment through its campaigns in the Alps, Corsica and Germany. In 1750, Dumas transferred to the colonial troops in Canada following the disbandment of his regiment the previous year. He was immediately given command of Fort Gaspareau for a year. He clearly enjoyed wilderness postings and quickly mastered the tactics peculiar to Canadian troops that, unlike many other French-born officers, he recognized as an important innovation. This attitude proved crucial to the French success on the banks of the Monongahela. **Captain François Le Marchand de Ligneris** was another experienced frontier officer whose first campaigns dated from the 1720s. An efficient leader as ever during the battle, he later became commandant of the French forces in the Ohio and led many successful raids against the British and Americans. His luck turned in 1759 when the force he led to relieve Fort Niagara was ambushed and he perished from his wounds. Although junior in rank, the role of **Ensign Charles-Michel Mouet de Langlade** in the battle of 9 July is now generally thought to have been greater than previously appreciated. He was related through his mother to some of the leading chiefs and was at home in both the Indian and the French

Robert Dinwiddie, although officially titled Lieutenant-Governor of Virginia, was its *de facto* governor from 1751 to 1758. The titular governor was the Earl of Albemarle whose post was a sinecure and who remained in England. As for Dinwiddie, he was determined to uphold Britain's claim to the Ohio Valley by any means available and was much more alarmed by the French presence in the Ohio Valley than governors of neighboring colonies.

Fort Presqu'Isle, c.1754. This bastioned fort was built of squared timber rather than of the usual structures of standing logs and earth usually put up by the French and English. From a 1930s painting by J.M. Plavcan. (Erie Maritime Museum, Erie, Pennsylvania. Author's photo)

cultures. As a result his influence over Indian nations of the Great Lakes area was considerable and his understanding of both the advantages and limitations of native diplomacy and warfare made him invaluable as an "Indian" leader. He apparently conceived the ambush plan used by de Beaujeu and Dumas.

The senior French commandant in the Ohio was **Captain Le Gardeur de Saint-Pierre**, who was succeeded by **Captain Pierre de Contrecoeur** who arrived in the area in April 1754. Both were experienced frontier soldiers. From 1752, their commander-in-chief was Governor General the **Marquis de Duquesne**, replaced in 1755 by the Canadian-born **Marquis de Vaudreuil** after his successful term as governor of Louisiana. Vaudreuil thoroughly understood and promoted the Canadian style of warfare, both on the frontier and for skirmishing in battles fought in a more conventional European tactical style.

INDIAN

The **Half-King** (Tanaghrisson) is the best known Indian involved in the events of 1754 in the Ohio Valley. He was chief of the Seneca Iroquois in the upper Ohio Valley and sided with the Virginians in their dispute with the French. He accompanied Washington to Fort Le Bœuf and, with about 20 warriors, was present at Jumonville Glen where he is said to have killed Jumonville. He later withdrew his approximately 80 warriors as Coulon de Villiers' force approached Fort Necessity. Sickly, he died in October 1754.

As events unfolded in 1755, the leaders of several nations rallied to the French. In June 1755, as Braddock's army slowly approached, such chiefs as **Pucksinwah**, **Athanese**, **White Eyes** and **Pontiac** (who would later gain immortal fame) could be found with their warriors at Fort Duquesne. Although there is hardly any record of the actions of these and other chiefs in the battle, their influence at command level was fundamental. The battle's outcome, so disastrous for the British and Americans, proves this.

Historic plaque at the site of Fort Presqu'Isle at Erie, Pennsylvania, near the shore of Lake Erie. The flags of the United States and Britain are visible but the flag of France has been taken down. This was in April 2003 during the second Iraq war. (Author's photo)

The creek at the site Fort Le Bœuf (now Waterford, Pennsylvania) built by the French in 1753. Washington described it as having "four houses [which] compose the sides; the Bastions are made of Piles driven into the Ground, and about 12 feet above, and sharp at Top, with Port Holes cut for Cannon and Loop Holes for the small Arms to fire through. There are eight 6 lb. pieces mounted, two in each Bastion, and one Piece of four Pound before the Gate; in the Bastions are a Guard House, Chapel, Doctor's Lodging, and the Commander's private store, round which are laid Eight Forms for the Cannon and Men to stand on; There are several barracks without the Fort, for the Soldiers Dwelling, covered, some with Bark, and some with Boards, and made chiefly, such as Stables, Smith's Shop, Etc." (Author's photo)

BRITISH

Captain James McKay, who commanded the first British regular troops in the Ohio Valley, could barely tolerate Washington's Virginians and was captured at Fort Necessity. **Major-General Edward Braddock** joined the Coldstream Guards in 1710 and served in Flanders at Flushing (British name for Vlissingen) but took no part in the fighting itself. In 1753 he left the Guards to become Colonel of the 14th Foot at Gibraltar. He was acting governor of the Rock and, in April 1754, was promoted to major-general. Appointed commander of the expedition to occupy the Ohio Valley in September, he was back in England in November and sailed for North America in January 1755. Once back in the colonies, he was anxious to get the campaign underway and brushed aside most American suggestions, such as strangling French communications by capturing Fort Niagara. This was not really feasible as he had his direct orders to occupy the Ohio and he accordingly moved west to Will's Creek, renamed it Fort Cumberland and made it his base of operations. His soldierly self-confidence was more tragically at fault, as events proved, when he dismissed warnings from colonial Americans to beware of the tactics practiced by the French and Indians. He was 60 years old when he led the army towards Fort Duquesne. Of his character, George Washington later wrote that he "was brave even to a fault and in regular service would have done honor to his profession. His attachments were warm, his enmities were strong, and having no disguise about him, both appeared in full force. He was generous and disinterested, but plain and blunt in his manner even to rudeness." A major in the 22nd Foot, **Sir John St Clair** won the coveted office of Deputy Quarter Master General of the British forces, no doubt because he had "much merit and great knowledge in military Affairs" as Governor Dinwiddie put it. It proved true during the campaign, which he survived. He went on to serve in the 60th Foot. **Sir Peter Halket**, Colonel of the 44th Foot and a veteran of

Major George Washington delivering the summons from Virginia Governor Dinwiddie to Commandant de Contrecoeur at Fort Le Bœuf in December 1753. The statue is at Waterford, Pennsylvania, site of Fort Le Bœuf. (Author's photo)

the 1745 Highland Rebellion, was by seniority second in command at the battle. He played no command role in the action, however, being in charge of the baggage where he perished along with his youngest son. **Colonel Thomas Dunbar**, commander of the 48th Foot, was left behind with the slow-moving wagons to set up camp not far from Great Meadows, while Braddock pressed ahead towards Fort Duquesne and his fate. Following the disaster of 9 July, Colonel Dunbar found himself the senior surviving officer of the battered army. The hurried retreat of his troops to Fort Cumberland might be understandable but his continued withdrawal to set up "winter quarters" in Philadelphia during August has been justly condemned by his contemporaries.

AMERICAN

George Washington, a young Virginian in his early 20s, was one of the central characters in this campaign. He was destined to play a key role in the founding of the United States of America, become an icon of democratic government and one of the best-known individuals in the modern world. His later fame, as a revered individual in his country and a universally respected statesman, has always made the study of his role in the controversial Jumonville incident awkward. Born on 22 February 1732 to a planter's family in Westmorland County, Virginia, young Washington had minimal schooling but showed exceptional skills in mathematics. This led him to become a surveyor of new territories in western Virginia when only 15. In 1752 he inherited the Mount Vernon plantation when his older brother Lawrence died. He quickly came to the attention of Virginia Governor Robert Dinwiddie who gave him the task of delivering a summons to the French in the newly built Fort Le Bœuf, which he did in December 1753. He held, at that time, the rank of major in the Virginia Militia and was colonel by the following year. After the Monongahela campaign he continued to command the Virginia Provincial Regiment until the French evacuated the Ohio. He then returned to managing his plantation until, in 1775, he was called to become the colonists' military leader in their struggle for independence from Britain, which they finally won in 1783. In 1789, Washington became the first president of the United States and served in that capacity until 1797. He died on 14 December 1799 at Mount Vernon.

Of other American colonists involved in the campaign, the frontiersman **Christopher Gist** was an indispensable guide to Major Washington and General Braddock. **Captain Robert Stobo** of the Virginia Regiment was left at Fort Duquesne as a hostage following the capture of Fort Necessity in 1754. Via a friendly Indian, he managed to sneak out a detailed plan of the fort, which was found in General Braddock's papers on the field of Monongahela on 9 July 1755. He was condemned to death but the sentence was never carried out and he eventually escaped.

OPPOSING ARMIES

THE FRENCH

A more accurate definition of the "French and Indians" of British and American histories might be "Canadians, French and Indians". From the end of the 17th century, the garrison of New France consisted of independent companies of regular colonial troops known as *Compagnies franches de la Marine*. The French Ministry of the Navy was responsible for the administration of colonies in America, hence "de la Marine". In 1754, Canada had a garrison of 30 colonial infantry companies, each with an establishment of 50 officers, cadets and enlisted men although in reality strength was always lower. In 1754, the official establishment of 1,500 NCOs and soldiers was short of some 500 men and that shortfall increased to 700 a year later. From 1750, Canada also possessed a regular colonial artillery company, the "Canonniers-Bombardiers", whose gunners were detached to various towns and forts. Louisiana had 35 infantry companies, six of which were posted in Illinois. Detachments of these troops were sent to the Ohio Valley from the upper Mississippi garrisons. The private soldiers of these regular troops were enlisted in France and sent to serve in North America. The bulk of these French regulars were unsuited to the wilderness and acted as regular garrisons in towns and forts. Around a quarter took to the ways of the forest, however, and were fit to participate in the long-distance expeditions

The meeting of French Creek and the Allegheny River, now at Franklin, Pennsylvania. The site of Fort Machault, also called Venango, was several hundred yards to the south. The two routes used by the French to travel south from Canada to Fort Duquesne on the Ohio River met at Fort Machault. (Author's photo)

The meeting of the Monongahela (left) and Allegheny (right) rivers which, united, form the Ohio River. The Virginians started building a fort at this point in 1754 until chased away by the French who then built Fort Duquesne on the spot. Its outline can be seen just in front of the fountain. Today it is a park in the very heart of the city of Pittsburgh. (Author's photo)

led by a selection of their Canadian officers. In theory, the rank system of officers of the *Compagnies franches* went no higher than captain. In fact the governor general, who exercised overall command, appointed the senior captains as commandants of an area or a fort. He would also appoint commandants to lead allied Indians, this role being reserved for officers with great experience and diplomacy in relations with the Indian nations.[1]

By the middle of the 18th century, the great majority of the officers were Canadian-born descendents of regular officers who had settled in Canada during the 17th century. The sons of officers often served as cadets with the troops until they could secure a commission. Thus, a powerful network of military families with close links in the fur trade dominated Canadian society. Most of the Canadian officers were familiar with frontier warfare and had often spent years serving in outposts in the wilderness. Many had learned Indian languages from the time they were cadets detached to serve and live with allied Indian nations.

While traveling back to Williamsburg from Fort Le Bœuf in late 1753, Major George Washington and veteran frontier trader Christopher Gist "fell in with a Party of French Indians, who had lain in wait for us; one of them fired at Mr. Gist or me, not 15 Steps, but fortunately missed. We took this Fellow into Custody, and kept him till about 9 o'clock at Night, and then let him go" according to Washington's journal.

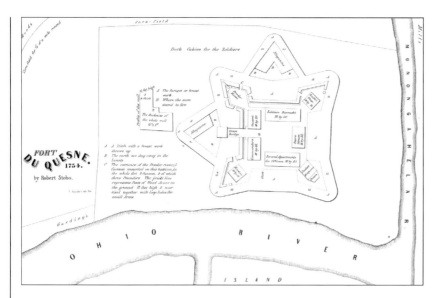

Plan of Fort Duquesne in 1754 by Robert Stobo. The remarkably detailed plan shows the fort's ramparts still under construction on the sides of the Ohio and Monongahela rivers. Print after Robert Stobo.

From their observations of Indian warfare and their way of life, Canadian officers devised an unwritten tactical doctrine that combined the best elements of European organization and discipline with the Indian's extraordinary ability to travel great distances largely undetected and mount very fierce surprise attacks. From the last decades of the 17th century mixed parties of Canadian militiamen and allied Indians put these tactics to the test. They were led by a cadre of selected regular officers, almost always Canadians, assisted by officer cadets and those regular soldiers who were experienced in the ways of the wilderness. This doctrine was an outstanding success; not only did it keep the colonists of the British colonies at bay but, just as important, it gave the French military superiority over hostile Indian nations. First the Iroquois Confederation, and especially its Mohawk nation, was humbled and later the Fox nation was almost annihilated in the southern Great Lakes area. This ensured that, from their string of forts on the shores of the Great Lakes and the upper Mississippi Valley, the French enjoyed substantial control over a vast area of North America's wilderness.

The settled areas of Canada, along the St Lawrence River, also had a centralized and very effective militia organization. Every able-bodied male colonist between the ages of 16 and 60 was enlisted in his parish's company. According to a 1750 muster, there were 165 militia companies gathering 724 officers, 498 sergeants and 11,687 militiamen. Many Canadians were employed in the fur trade as voyageurs or as small traders, either part-time of full-time, and thus made ideal candidates for wilderness expeditions when called up for militia duty. In 1755 for instance, 24 of the 83 men in the Côte Saint-Michel company in Montréal were reported on duty out west, mostly in the Ohio Valley or Illinois. Such individuals usually came from the Montréal district, where over half of the colony's population lived, and were reputed to be a rowdy and undisciplined group of men, but also the best militiamen in the colony. As they handled guns from childhood, many were outstanding marksmen with their favorite weapon, the lightweight and dependable smoothbore hunting and trade musket made in Tulle, France. A key difference between the Canadian militia and the militias of the American colonies was that the former operated under

Captain Jean-Daniel Dumas, the "hero of the Monongahela" who ably took command of the mixed French, Canadian and Indian force early in the battle, following the death of Beaujeu. This portrait shows Dumas wearing the all-blue coat laced with gold of a *Maréchal de Camp* (Major General), a rank he achieved in 1780. The words "Isle de France" on the map beside him refer to his term as governor, from 1767 to 1774, of Isle de France (now called Mauritius) in the Indian Ocean.

Captain Daniel-Hyacinthe Lienhart de Beaujeu. He commanded the French and Indian force but was killed at the beginning of the battle of the Monongahela on 9 July 1755.

a highly effective central command system. Whatever the governor general decided was the order of the day; there was no debate, and Canadian militiamen came out wearing their own clothes and carrying, for the most part, their own arms and equipment. In the summer, this might only consist of a shirt, a breechclout, mitasses, moccasins, a Tulle musket, several knives, and a tomahawk. They were often taken to be "dressed as Indians" by the Anglo-Americans. They were not paid, only fed on duty, but might pick up extra money from some captured booty or by being employed in construction as well as conducting trade with the Indians as a sideline. All were familiar with the basic principles of Canadian tactics. If properly led, and they usually were by experienced officers, these tough and hardy men constituted one of the best auxiliary forces to be found anywhere in the world.

THE INDIANS

The Indian allies of the French have long been represented as subordinate auxiliaries; in reality they were quite independent, not only as nations but as individuals. They actually were more individual warriors within an Indian nation's sub-grouping. They operated in groups of varying sizes that formed and dissolved at a moment's notice. Their war chiefs might have great influence but had no real power to conduct operations in the same way a European officer could; individual warriors ultimately determined in what circumstances they would deploy. Since the 17th century, French diplomacy towards the Indian nations skillfully and patiently took into account the various needs of the native nations while gaining the trust of many of them. The French were also much more "present" within the tribes than the Anglo-Americans thanks to their fur traders, missionaries and officers who went deep into the wilderness where the Indians were, and often lived in their villages. Thus, many Indians came to acknowledge "Onontio" – the governor general of New France – as their "Great Father". Indian chiefs were honored with elaborate "officers' commissions", such as that given to Iroquois chief Dgichekégée, as well as silver medals, gorgets, guns and clothing for their warriors. Although they at first resented the building of French forts in the Ohio and complained of it to Captain Marin, the "Loups" (Delawares), the "Chaouanons", and the Seneca Iroquois mostly rallied to the skillful and considerate French officer/diplomat as did other warriors from farther away such as the Illinois, Potawatamies and Ottawa nations.

There were relatively few Indians favorably inclined to the Anglo-Americans, the best known being the Half-King and the Iroquois warriors in the Ohio who followed him. Once Braddock arrived on the scene with his regulars, Indian alliances did not seem so important …

The British arriving from Europe were full of self-confidence and prejudices against the North American "savages". Virginians, especially those familiar with the frontier, knew better what they were up against. As Captain Steven of the Virginia Rangers wrote: "formal attacks & platoon firing would never answer against the savages and Canadians. It ought to be laid down as a maxim to attack them first, to fight them in their own way, and go against them light & naked, as they come against us, creeping near and hunting us as they would do a herd of buffaloes or deer; whereas you might as well send a cow in pursuit of a hare as an English soldier loaded in their way with a coat, jacket, &c, &c, &c, after Canadians in their shirts, who can shoot and run well, or naked Indians accustomed to the woods."

THE BRITISH AND AMERICANS

At the time of the French advance to secure the Ohio Valley, there were very few British regular troops in the old "Thirteen Colonies". To defend Lake Champlain, Lake Ontario and New York City there were but four independent companies in the colony of New York, with three more in South Carolina to guard against potential Spanish and Indian forays. The "Fourteenth Colony", Nova Scotia, and Newfoundland had three regular regiments with artillery and ranger companies as they had as their neighbor the powerful French naval base and fortress of Louisbourg on Cape Breton Island. In addition there were the French forts Beauséjour and Gaspareau right on their western borders and most of its population were neutral Acadians, the descendants of the settlers of French Acadia before it was ceded to Great Britain in 1713. In all, the Anglo-American colonies had about 2,500 British regular troops of variable quality in 1754.

The first British regular troops in the Ohio Valley were detachments from the three South Carolina independent companies formed into the temporary Independent Company led by Captain McKay that joined Washington's Virginians at Fort Necessity in June 1754. Another detachment from the New York Independent Companies arrived too late to influence events. Used to garrison duty, these troops were quite unsuited to the frontier and, in any event, were too few to face the French regulars. The two British regular infantry regiments sent to North America were Colonel Sir Peter Halket's 44th and Colonel Thomas Dunbar's 48th. These regiments each had an establishment of 700 men that came over from the United Kingdom but they were to recruit 300 more in North America. Recruiting proved most disappointing and Dunbar's 48th was even below its initial establishment when it marched west in June 1755. They were accompanied by a company of the Royal Artillery under Captain Ord to serve the field guns of the expedition. In preparation for the expedition, General Braddock ordered that soldiers leave behind their hangers (short swords), belts and heavy equipment, and bring only a spare shirt, a pair of spare stockings, a pair of spare shoes and wear only their brown marching gaiters. They were issued new clothing that included "Osnabrig" linen waistcoat and breeches rather than those made of warm red wool as "the excessive heat would have made the otages insupportable" noted Orme. But no bush warfare training was provided. On the whole, these were good troops but they were totally unprepared and untrained for the kind of fighting they would face in the wilderness.

The American colonial forces overwhelmingly consisted of men listed on the militia rolls as able to bear arms. Each colony, except Pennsylvania which was governed by the pacifist Quakers, had a militia organization whose effectiveness varied considerably from one colony to another. Some colonies had a few good units of well-armed and uniformed volunteer

Charles Le Moyne, Baron de Longueuil, interim governor general of New France during 1752–53. An experienced frontier colonial officer from one of Canada's most influential and distinguished families, he favored securing the Ohio route. (Musée d'art de Joliette, Joliette, Québec)

A senior officer of the *Compagnies franches de la Marine*, the colonial regular troops stationed in New France, c.1750s. There is no known likeness of Captain Jacques Le Gardeur de Saint-Pierre described by Washington as "an elderly gentleman with much the air of a soldier" when he met him at Fort Le Bœuf in late November 1753. Saint-Pierre passed away in Montréal in September 1755 and the inventory of his belongings reveals he had much the same dress as shown in this illustration by Eugène Lelièpvre. This included a "half worn" uniform coat, a blue waistcoat laced with gold and an half-beaver hat edged with gold lace. Like most senior officers, de Saint-Pierre was a knight of the royal and military order of Saint-Louis and would have worn the knight's cross hung on a scarlet silk ribbon as shown. (Parks Canada)

cavalry, frontier patrols and artillery but, on the whole, the colonial American militias were untrained and poorly armed. The colony of Virginia, which took the lead in opposing the French in the Ohio Valley, had a militia estimated at about 36,000 men able to bear arms, but to quote a period report, "not above half that number are armed, and the arms of those who have any are of different bores". In an effort to prepare it for duty, Governor Robert Dinwiddie had, in November 1753, divided the Virginia Militia into four districts and sent in "adjutants" to "teach the officers their duty and train the private men to the use of arms."[2] Obviously, as good a measure as it was, this would not be enough and, in January 1754, the Virginia legislature authorized funds to raise two provincial companies of 100 men each and these were later joined by more companies to form the Virginia provincial regiment. This quickly grew to six companies by March, organized as a regiment under Colonel Joshua Fry and Lieutenant-Colonel Washington. The uniform was "a Coat and Breeches of red Cloth". This changed to "blue turned up with red" from February 1755 for Virginia provincial companies that served with General Braddock's army.[3]

American colonial provincial troops were made up of officers and men enlisted for full-time service, usually from early spring to late fall. The Virginia provincials raised in the spring of 1754, and involved in the Jumonville ambush and at Fort Necessity, were disbanded in the fall, as was the custom. For the 1755 campaign, General Braddock preferred companies of rangers, carpenters, or pioneers and light horse. In terms of tactics, the militias and provincials mostly served as support to the British regulars; their rangers and light troops could to an extent check the marauding frontier raids of the French and Indians, but could not make forays deep into the wilderness. American provincial infantry regiments were generally not as disciplined, nor as well-drilled or as steady in action as British regular troops. Provincial officers lacked military education and experience in the field. All this surprised no one as these were temporary units best suited for support or garrison duty. On the other hand, Alexander Hamilton and others noted the "courage of our Americans demonstrates that they would make excellent soldiers." Some would gain considerable experience and distinction during the Seven Years War, but in 1754–55 American provincials and militias were very new to the art of war as waged in North America. For the vast majority of Americans at that time, safety resided in the extensively settled farming areas, fishing villages and towns found all along the Atlantic seaboard. It ended at the edge of the continent's primeval forest wilderness; that was the domain of their "French and Indian" opponents.

1 There were also a few administrative staff officers with the rank of major in New France, notably that of town major in the main garrison towns (Québec, Montréal, Trois-Rivières, Louisbourg, New Orleans and the Illinois) and a staff "major of the troops" usually serving on the staff of the governor general at Québec. The engineers were the other principal staff officers in Canada, Louisbourg and Louisiana and the captain of the usually largely fictitious guard of the governor general would act as his aide-de-camp.
2 WO 34/101.
3 This first Virginia Regiment raised in early 1754 and disbanded in the fall had a red uniform. It was apparently quite simple without lapels or lace for the men although the officers' seemed to have been scarlet with gold lace. The Virginia Regiment raised in September 1755 under Colonel Washington wore these colors with silver lace for officers. Brock, *Official Records of Robert Dinwiddie*, Vol. 1; see also Chartrand, René, *Colonial American Troops 1610–1774 (1)* (Osprey Men-at-Arms Series No. 366) for further details and illustrations on this topic.

OPPOSING PLANS

The initial French plan, which had been recommended since the late 1740s but was only decisively implemented, with the blessing of the royal court, by Governor General Duquesne, was to physically occupy the Ohio Valley with a string of forts. The troops posted there with their Indian allies would secure the area and chase out any intruding Anglo-American traders and settlers. Although the forts were built during 1753 and 1754, French senior authorities had no preconceived and approved plan beyond this. Although the forts were excellent bases for potential raids deep into settled areas of Virginia, Maryland and Pennsylvania, France and Britain were not at war and as such there were no plans to carry out anything of that nature. The fact that both countries had rather strained peacetime relations had been a fact of life since the Middle Ages and was nothing new. At this point the French simply wanted to deny the Ohio Valley to their British opponents. No plans existed to escalate the conflict beyond this.

But conflict there would be for the British had no intention of abandoning their claim to the Ohio, as expressed by the Governor of Virginia, simply because the French had built forts and physically occupied the valley. To uphold their claim, the Virginians would have to raise troops, construct roads to the Monongahela River and, with a train of artillery, besiege and take Fort Duquesne. Provincial troops were raised and did indeed move into the area, which led to the Jumonville Incident in May 1754. Within weeks the French and Indians, who were far superior to the Anglo-Americans in wilderness warfare, had taken Fort Necessity and avenged Jumonville. When news of this reached Europe, both France and Britain sent troops to North America in the spring of 1755. Of the six French battalions sent as reinforcements to New France, four landed in Québec and two in Louisbourg. Both destinations were a long way from the Ohio and there would not be enough time to get these troops to Fort Duquesne. Furthermore, transporting sufficient supplies over such long distances down the Ohio valley to feed any large body of troops was practically impossible. There were thus severe logistical and time constraints on what the French could do. Despite being heavily outnumbered, their plan was simply to hold on to the Ohio any way they could, but there was no clear plan of how to do this. Their greatest advantages were probably their Indian allies and their proficiency in wilderness warfare.

By contrast the two regular British regiments sent to Virginia under General Braddock would, despite having to pass through some wilderness, be within striking distance of Fort Duquesne in a relatively short time. From Williamsburg, Virginia, the army would march to the fork of the Potomac River at Will's Creek, Maryland (named Fort Cumberland by General Braddock). Ahead was mountainous country. Moving west, the troops would cross the Cumberland Gap of the Allegheny Mountains and

This portrait, said to be of Major-General Edward Braddock, started appearing in late 19th century publications and has been used ever since as his likeness. The head may indeed be Braddock's but the coat's cut and its epaulets are obvious embellishments dating from much later, as nothing like this was worn by generals in the mid-18th century British army. An original portrait of Braddock has yet to be found.

Major-General Edward Braddock as interpreted from the earlier print by artist Lucille W. Hitchcock for Woodrow Wilson's article on George Washington published in *Harper's New Monthly Magazine* in March 1896. A tricorn has been added but the uniform with large epaulets remains.

Sir John St Clair, Deputy Quartermaster General of Braddock's army. He was wounded during the battle of the Monongahela but escaped and recovered. He went on to serve as a field officer in the 60th Foot (Royal Americans) during the remainder of the war. Portrait by Allan Ramsay. (Fort Ligonier Museum, Ligonier, Pennsylvania. Author's photo)

emerge at Little Meadows. They would now find themselves in true wilderness and the march would continue to Great Meadows and the site of Fort Necessity. From there it was several days' march to reach the twisting Monongahela River. Crossing to the north bank of the river they would be some seven to eight miles from their objective – Fort Duquesne. Once the fort was reached, a perimeter would be established, trenches and batteries built and, after some sustained bombardment, it was hoped that the garrison would surrender. Fort Duquesne was, after all, only an earth and timber construction unlikely to resist the cannons and mortars the British had dragged through the wilderness for very long. If the garrison stubbornly held out, an assault by the two British regiments would finish the job. After this success, the Anglo-American army would move north and take the French forts right up to Lake Erie.

Braddock and his officers were certainly mindful that the army might come under attack or find itself in some sort of ambush in the wilderness. Right up to the moment when the battle of the Monongahela started, Braddock's column was always preceded by a vanguard of rangers and light cavalry and a screen of skirmishers operated on either flank of the column some way into the woods. These were sensible precautions and more than would be expected of most commanders in Europe; they testify that Braddock was indeed mindful of "surprises" by the French and Indians. However, the reality was that in the wilderness his army was actually totally blind at anything beyond a few hundred yards. There were no long-range scouts to provide Braddock with precise information on the enemy's forces and the nature of the terrain ahead. Nevertheless, the force marching on Fort Duquesne was certainly formidable; nothing like it had ever been seen on the frontier before and this filled Braddock with an optimism that gave some of the more cautious American officers with frontier experience, notably Washington, cause for concern. They knew how resilient and resourceful the French and Indians could be. To be fair to Braddock and his British officers, however, the warnings were vague and likely interpreted in terms of possible nuisances during skirmishes. No one, American or British, could foresee the unprecedented scale of the coming catastrophe. The British plan relied heavily on the doctrine of overwhelming force, which would inevitably sweep the Anglo-American force to its anticipated victory.

For their part, there was no coherent French master plan for confronting Braddock and his army once they knew that he was marching on Fort Duquesne. Equally no worthwhile battle plan could be drawn up before the day itself. The French soldiers and Canadian militiamen were considerably outnumbered and, with the fluid nature of alliances with the Indian nations, the crucial participation of allied Indians in any engagement could not be taken for granted. These realities faced by French frontier officers rendered any long-range detailed planning next to useless. The emphasis was on the ability to react swiftly and decisively to any vital intelligence that was received. This enthusiasm would usually carry the Indian allies along with the French commanders, ensuring they "took up the hatchet" against the intruding enemies. Once the participation of the Indian allies was guaranteed, and this would inevitably be within 24 hours of the opening of any engagement, only the most basic planning remained: meet the enemy, surround him and then pepper his column with a murderous fire from cover.

FROM JUMONVILLE GLEN TO THE MONONGAHELA

Washington on the offensive

The seizure by French troops of the fort Virginian soldiers were building at the junction of the Allegheny, Monongahela and Ohio rivers was intolerable to Governor Dinwiddie and many in the American colonies. It was seen as tantamount to an act of war on the part of the French. Major Washington was still in the area, at Will's Creek with about 150 Virginian soldiers. Following the Indian and traders' paths, Will's Creek was about 140 miles from Fort Duquesne. About halfway along this route was Redstone Creek where the Ohio Company had built a warehouse. Dinwiddie and Washington planned for the Virginia troops to assemble at Redstone Creek and, as far as possible, construct a road suitable for wagons and guns. A force would then be sent to dislodge the French from the forks at Fort Duquesne. At present, however, there were no supply wagons or horses, no additional troops, and no Indian allies.

Moving west from Will's Creek, Major Washington's talents as a surveyor proved useful for planning a road that would, on the whole, follow the Nemacolin trail made for the Ohio Company. This Indian trail had also been used by Anglo-American traders for years. The trail was named after Nemacolin, a Delaware Indian who had marked out the route to the west for the Virginians of the Ohio Company. Although Washington's plan required that he build a road about 100 miles long through some very difficult and mountainous terrain, he and his officers were determined to open the route to the Monongahela River. It was the only practicable way to transport the artillery necessary to overcome Fort Duquesne into the Ohio valley. Despite the strong French presence, the Virginians considered it vital that they maintain a presence on the frontier to sustain their claims in the Ohio and encourage their Indian allies.

The actual building of the road turned out to be a difficult and back-breaking labor for the Virginians. There was no easy, obvious route. Washington explored the possibility of following the Youghiogheny River, but any navigable route was blocked by falls that no craft could cross. The Virginians finally found an opening through the mountains, about a mile in length, called Great Meadows and established a temporary camp there. They could not have known the fame that future events would bring to this spot, although Washington prophetically described Great Meadows as "a charming field for an encounter".

By May 1754, the building of Fort Duquesne was nearly finished and Commandant de Contrecoeur sent out some French and Indian scouts towards the east. He knew the Virginians had to be somewhere out there and after a few days the scouts came back with worrisome news. According to them, the Virginians were building supply depots (this would have been the camp at Great Meadows) and the scouts felt it could only be in preparation for mounting an attack on Fort Duquesne. If this

Lieutenant-Colonel Thomas Gage, 44th Foot, commanded the vanguard that stumbled upon Beaujeu's force on 9 July 1755. His role at the beginning of the battle has been questioned: why did his scouts not spot the French and Indians until it was too late? On the other hand, Gage is reported to have displayed outstanding bravery during the battle. He later attained field rank and was commander-in-chief of British forces in North America between 1763 and 1775. Print after John Singleton Copley. (National Archives of Canada, C1347)

A private of the *Compagnies franches de la Marine* in the regulation uniform, c. 1750–57. The colonial regular troops stationed in New France were issued standard European style uniforms as shown in this reconstruction by Eugène Lelièpvre made from clothing bills and descriptions. The accoutrements consisted of a ventral cartridge box holding nine rounds with a reddish brown leather cover flap on a buff waistbelt also holding the sword and bayonet. The musket was usually the M1728 army musket or its marine version made in Tulle. This may have been the dress worn by Jumonville's detachment. Soldiers in wilderness outposts also used the much more practical "Canadian" costume on campaign but some sentries could also be seen at Fort Duquesne in 1754 wearing this "regulation uniform". Some may have also been in regulation uniform at the battle of the Monongahela. A British account mentioned that "the French were mostly in Indian the dress notwithstand[in]g several were seen in the French uniform." (Pargellis, *Military Affairs*, p. 117). (Parks Canada)

was true, de Contrecoeur faced something of a dilemma as France and Great Britain were not at war, although their North American colonies were clearly embroiled in a confrontation over the Ohio Valley. The best course of action seemed to be to send an officer with an ultimatum to be delivered to the first Anglo-American officer he encountered. This ultimatum would request that the intruders "leave in peace" and warn that there would be no more warnings. Should any hostile act occur, the Anglo-Americans would have to bear the responsibility as Contrecoeur fully intended to "maintain the existing union between two princes that are friends", referring to the kings of France and England. Whatever the particular plans of the English officer, Contrecoeur was confident that his envoy would enjoy every consideration and be sent back with an answer. Ensign Joseph Coulon de Villiers, Sieur de Jumonville was selected for the task. He was 36 years old and an experienced officer.

Jumonville's party departs for Great Meadows

On 23 May, Jumonville left Fort Duquesne, with an escort of 32 men including an interpreter, heading east towards Great Meadows bearing the ultimatum. A drummer named La Batterie was also part of the detachment. This appears to confirm that Jumonville was not leading a war party. A drummer was considered necessary to deliver an ultimatum according to the protocol in force amongst European armies at the time. As the party marched through the forest, the weather was rainy and unpleasant. It rained on 26 May and, seeking some cover from the elements, Jumonville's party settled down in a low spot below a rocky ridge deep in the forest, about five miles (8km) from Great Meadows and remained there the next day (27 May) as the weather conditions were not much better.

By this time, Major Washington had known for three days that a French party was approaching the area. It had been spotted by the Iroquois scouts of Chief Half-King who had warned Major Washington on 24 May. The following day he sent some scouts on horseback to patrol the area but they came back having seen no one. On 27 May, Christopher Gist arrived saying that a party of some 50 French had come to his settlement, had killed a cow and smashed everything in his dwelling. Major Washington at once detached a party of 75 Virginia soldiers to go to Gist's house. Then, at about eight in the evening, a messenger from the Half-King came to report that the French party was seemingly encamped in a nearby gully. In case it was a French trap, Major Washington had the ammunition in the camp at Great Meadows hidden and left a party to guard it. Then, accompanied by some 40 Virginians, he proceeded to meet the Half-King and they agreed that the Virginians and Indians would attack jointly. About 20 to 30 Indians joined Washington's men and all moved quietly through the forest to the spot where the French were believed to be. It was a difficult trek in the darkness; they nevertheless came silently to the rocky ridge overlooking the French encampment without being detected. The Virginians and Indians were now overlooking the French camp below.

Ambush

Precisely what happened next has never really been clearly established. Evidence, such as it is, is both scarce and contradictory. George Washington's version, as outlined in his *Remarks* on his early career, mentioned that "the French sent a detachment to reconnoiter our Camp and obtain intelligence of our strength & position [at Great Meadows]; notice of which being given by the [allied Indian] Scouts, G W [George Washington] marched at the head of the party, attacked, killed 9 or 10, & captured 20 odd." His report of 29 May to Virginia Governor Dinwiddie was written in a similar vein, stating that, in conjunction with the allied Indians of chiefs Half-King and Monacatuca, he had "form'd a disposition to attack on all sides, which we accordingly did, and after an engagement of about 15 minutes, we killed 10, wounded one and took 21 prisoners, amongst those that were killed, was Monsieur de Jumonville, the commander." One Virginian was killed in the fight. It was a remarkably brief account of a skirmish so significant that it led to a full-scale world war.

There are other accounts from witnesses but all are second or third hand. The one man in the French party that got away was a Canadian militiaman named Monceau, who delivered the first news of Jumonville's death. His was the version that Commandant de Contrecoeur wrote to Governor General Duquesne stating that in "the morning, at seven o'clock, they [the French] found they were surrounded by English on one side and Indians on the other. They received two volleys from the English, and none from the Indians. Through an interpreter M. de Jumonville told them to stop, as he had to speak to them. They [the English] stopped. M. de Jumonville had read to them my summons to retire … While it was being read, the said Monceau saw all our Frenchmen coming up behind M. de Jumonville, so that they formed a group in the midst of the English and Indians. Meanwhile, Monceau slipped to one side, and went off through the woods." The gunner "J.C.B." who was at Fort Duquesne at the time also obtained his version from Monceau who had "heard musket shots, and a few moments later, a second volley with cries of the dying" men. He concluded his party had been ambushed and defeated and decided to run

Colonel George Washington in the uniform of the Virginia Regiment. The coat is blue with scarlet lapels, cuffs and lining and scarlet waistcoat, silver buttons, lace and gorget, crimson sash over the shoulder. It is likely that Washington had a similar dress when serving as Braddock's American aide, as Virginia troops wore blue uniforms with scarlet facings from about February 1755. Washington sat for this portrait by C.W. Peale in 1772 wearing his old regimentals. It hangs in the chapel of the University of Washington and Lee in Virginia. (Author's photo)

A group of Canadian militiamen in the mid-18th century. On the left, a militiaman dressed in a blanket coat "capot" with "mitasses" Indian leggings, moccasins, waist sash and the cloth cap. Like most militiamen, he is armed with a light-caliber Tulle hunting musket, would have a tomahawk and carry up to three knives. The central figure is a militia officer whose rank is only recognizable by his gilt gorget and sword. In the background to the right a militiaman wears a short capot while his companion has one made of homespun. Reconstitution by Francis Back. (Parks Canada)

A light-caliber hunting musket made in Tulle, France. This type of musket was also used in the fur trade and was the firm favorite with Canadians and their Indian allies. Its caliber, as expressed in the 18th century, was "28 to the pound" which meant it took 28 balls of that caliber to make a pound of lead weight. The more balls it took to make the pound, the smaller they were and so was the caliber of the musket's barrel, or the fewer balls the larger the caliber. The musket shown has steel fittings, which was usual, the more expensive ones having brass fittings, and these might be decorated with engravings. This musket did not have a bayonet but this was of little significance as Canadians and Indians avoided hand-to-hand fighting as a rule and were adept with knife or tomahawk if circumstances required. (Parks Canada, Ottawa)

back to Fort Duquesne to bring news of the battle. By making detours in the forest to evade the British-allied Indians, he reached the fort six days later.[4]

A more direct witness of the event was Ensign Pierre-Jacques Drouillon, an officer captured by Washington's men. His version was given in English through a translated letter to Governor Dinwiddie in which he stated that Washington should have taken notice, when he attacked, at "about 7 or 8 o'Clock in the morning", that the French detachment did not take "to our arms: he [Washington] might have heard our Interpreter [call out] … instead of taking that opportunity to fire upon us." Although Drouillon was part of the French detachment, and his recollection is thus essentially first-hand, he was not with the interpreter and as such his account must involve some supposition.[5]

In Fort Duquesne, de Contrecoeur, hearing of the incident, made a rough note on his copy of the summons that Jumonville had been killed by the English while reading it. Amongst those killed by the Virginian's volleys was the drummer and this would seem to add credence to the assertion that Jumonville tried to read the summons. De Contrecoeur received another message, this time from La Chauvignerie who commanded an out-post at Chiningue (Logstown, near Ambridge, Pennsylvania), that allied Indians had reported the killing of Jumonville and many of his men while the summons was being read. The Indians further said they saved the other French from being killed by intervening to stop the shooting. However, this must have been hearsay because no French-allied Indians are known to have been with Jumonville's party. The Indians were not above inventing some facts to gain favor.[6]

Whatever actually happened, the results of the "Jumonville incident" would prove to be seismic in their consequences. Perhaps Governor Dinwiddie foresaw the explosive impact the incident would have when the news reached Versailles and London. In his dispatch relating the event, he tried to reassure ministers that Washington's engagement had been "a little skirmish [that] was really the work of the Half-King and … [his] Indians. We were but auxiliaries to them …"!

FORT NECESSITY

Following his victory over Jumonville's party, Washington and his men returned to nearby Great Meadows. While very pleased by his success, Washington felt that a "fort of necessity" should be built at Great Meadows as a more secure base and for protection against the probable French retaliation. Situated near modern-day Farmington, Pennsylvania, Fort Necessity, as it came to be called, was a small circular log palisade with trenches covering some two thirds of its exterior.

The first major consequence of Jumonville's ambush by the Virginians occurred at Fort Duquesne. As soon as Commandant de Contrecoeur

JUMONVILLE GLEN AND FORT NECESSITY

27 May 1754, viewed from the southeast, showing the attack on Ensign de Jumonville's party on 27 May and the capture of Fort Necessity on 3 July 1754.

Note: Gridlines are shown at intervals of 1/2 mile/0.8km

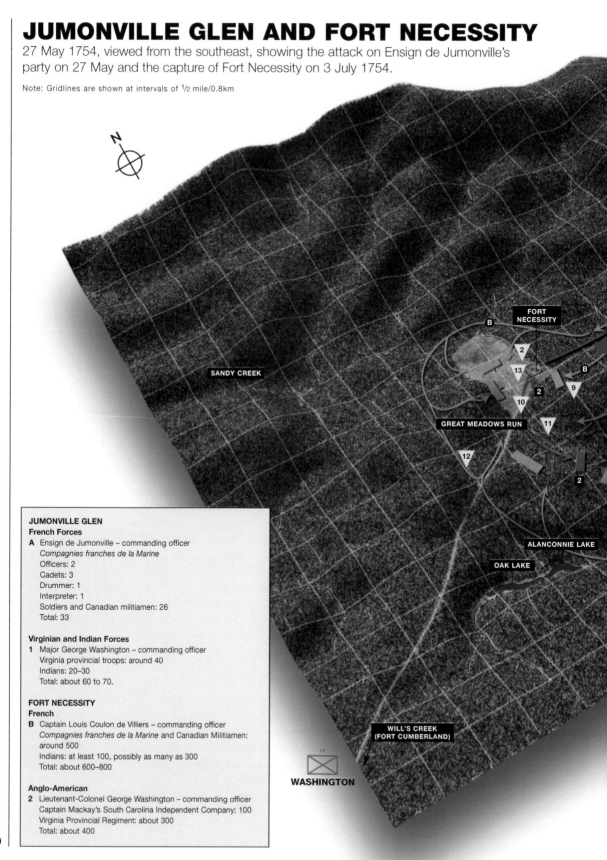

SANDY CREEK

FORT NECESSITY

B

2

13

B

2

9

10

GREAT MEADOWS RUN

11

12

2

ALANCONNIE LAKE

OAK LAKE

**WILL'S CREEK
(FORT CUMBERLAND)**

WASHINGTON

JUMONVILLE GLEN
French Forces
A   Ensign de Jumonville – commanding officer
     Compagnies franches de la Marine
     Officers: 2
     Cadets: 3
     Drummer: 1
     Interpreter: 1
     Soldiers and Canadian militiamen: 26
     Total: 33

Virginian and Indian Forces
1   Major George Washington – commanding officer
     Virginia provincial troops: around 40
     Indians: 20–30
     Total: about 60 to 70.

FORT NECESSITY
French
B   Captain Louis Coulon de Villiers – commanding officer
     Compagnies franches de la Marine and Canadian Militiamen:
     around 500
     Indians: at least 100, possibly as many as 300
     Total: about 600–800

Anglo-American
2   Lieutenant-Colonel George Washington – commanding officer
     Captain Mackay's South Carolina Independent Company: 100
     Virginia Provincial Regiment: about 300
     Total: about 400

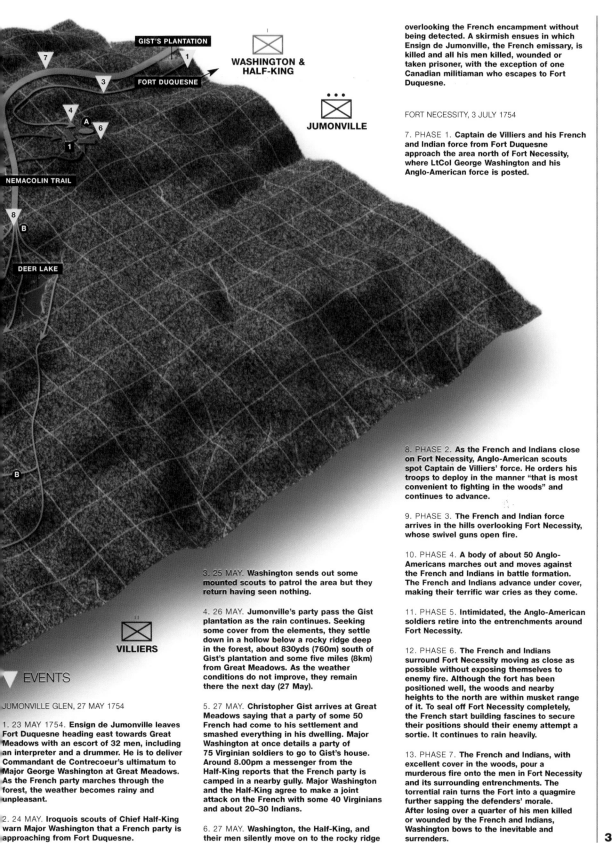

GIST'S PLANTATION

WASHINGTON &
HALF-KING

FORT DUQUESNE

JUMONVILLE

NEMACOLIN TRAIL

DEER LAKE

VILLIERS

overlooking the French encampment without being detected. A skirmish ensues in which Ensign de Jumonville, the French emissary, is killed and all his men killed, wounded or taken prisoner, with the exception of one Canadian militiaman who escapes to Fort Duquesne.

FORT NECESSITY, 3 JULY 1754

7. PHASE 1. **Captain de Villiers and his French and Indian force from Fort Duquesne approach the area north of Fort Necessity, where LtCol George Washington and his Anglo-American force is posted.**

8. PHASE 2. **As the French and Indians close on Fort Necessity, Anglo-American scouts spot Captain de Villiers' force. He orders his troops to deploy in the manner "that is most convenient to fighting in the woods" and continues to advance.**

9. PHASE 3. **The French and Indian force arrives in the hills overlooking Fort Necessity, whose swivel guns open fire.**

10. PHASE 4. **A body of about 50 Anglo-Americans marches out and moves against the French and Indians in battle formation. The French and Indians advance under cover, making their terrific war cries as they come.**

11. PHASE 5. **Intimidated, the Anglo-American soldiers retire into the entrenchments around Fort Necessity.**

12. PHASE 6. **The French and Indians surround Fort Necessity moving as close as possible without exposing themselves to enemy fire. Although the fort has been positioned well, the woods and nearby heights to the north are within musket range of it. To seal off Fort Necessity completely, the French start building fascines to secure their positions should their enemy attempt a sortie. It continues to rain heavily.**

13. PHASE 7. **The French and Indians, with excellent cover in the woods, pour a murderous fire onto the men in Fort Necessity and its surrounding entrenchments. The torrential rain turns the Fort into a quagmire further sapping the defenders' morale. After losing over a quarter of his men killed or wounded by the French and Indians, Washington bows to the inevitable and surrenders.**

3. 25 MAY. **Washington sends out some mounted scouts to patrol the area but they return having seen nothing.**

4. 26 MAY. **Jumonville's party pass the Gist plantation as the rain continues. Seeking some cover from the elements, they settle down in a hollow below a rocky ridge deep in the forest, about 830yds (760m) south of Gist's plantation and some five miles (8km) from Great Meadows. As the weather conditions do not improve, they remain there the next day (27 May).**

5. 27 MAY. **Christopher Gist arrives at Great Meadows saying that a party of some 50 French had come to his settlement and smashed everything in his dwelling. Major Washington at once details a party of 75 Virginian soldiers to go to Gist's house. Around 8.00pm a messenger from the Half-King reports that the French party is camped in a nearby gully. Major Washington and the Half-King agree to make a joint attack on the French with some 40 Virginians and about 20–30 Indians.**

6. 27 MAY. **Washington, the Half-King, and their men silently move on to the rocky ridge**

EVENTS

JUMONVILLE GLEN, 27 MAY 1754

1. 23 MAY 1754. **Ensign de Jumonville leaves Fort Duquesne heading east towards Great Meadows with an escort of 32 men, including an interpreter and a drummer. He is to deliver Commandant de Contrecoeur's ultimatum to Major George Washington at Great Meadows. As the French party marches through the forest, the weather becomes rainy and unpleasant.**

2. 24 MAY. **Iroquois scouts of Chief Half-King warn Major Washington that a French party is approaching from Fort Duquesne.**

31

A highly decorated commission given by the French governors to Indian chiefs. Such commissions were given to some chiefs in the Ohio Valley. This example was given by the governor of Louisiana, Louis de Kerlérec to Cherokee Chief Okana-Stoté and was dated at New Orleans on 27 February 1761. Meant to impress and rally the leaders of allied Indian nations, these commissions were quite ornate. The full coat-of-arms of France appear above the arms of Louisiana and those of the governor who is pictured below with the chief. (United States National Archives)

learned of the ambush from militiaman Monceau, he at once wrote of the event to Governor General Duquesne at Québec and, with the resources available to him at Fort Duquesne, immediately set about organizing a strong force to go after the Virginians who had killed Jumonville and his men. Within a few days, de Contrecoeur had collected a force of some 500 French soldiers and Canadian militiamen, along with a few Indians, who were prepared to move east. The command of the party was given to artillery Captain Le Mercier. However, on the morning of 26 June, a convoy of canoes and boats arrived at Fort Duquesne. It was Captain Louis Coulon de Villiers, an experienced frontier officer who also held the title of commandant of the Indians in the area, with some 300 Indians accompanying about 50 French soldiers and Canadian militiamen bringing supplies for Fort Duquesne. As soon as he landed, Captain de Villiers learned of de Jumonville's death and its circumstances. He was deeply grieved, shocked and angered at the news: de Jumonville was his younger brother. As he was senior to Captain Le Mercier, de Villiers immediately asked Commandant de Contrecoeur to allow him to command the expedition preparing to march against the Virginians. This was certainly within de Villiers' prerogatives as a senior officer. Commandant de Contrecoeur agreed as, in addition, de Villiers might be able to persuade the Indians to join him.

De Contrecoeur's and de Villiers' first action was indeed to summon a war council with the Indian chiefs on 27 June. De Contrecoeur had the respect and confidence of many chiefs; they knew he had influence and spoke to and for "Onontio", the Great Father at Québec – the governor general of New France. As he gave wampum belts, he spoke to the gathered chiefs, whom he addressed as "children" in the name of the Great Father, of Onontio's summons for the English to leave the area in peace, that the English had instead assassinated the officer sent to tell them, and that he had put Captain de Villiers in command of the expedition. De Villiers, the "commandant of the Indians", wished "with all his heart" to avenge the death of his brother, the young Jumonville.

Back view of a "Canadian Warrior", almost naked except for tattoos and warpaint all over his body. He wears ornate belts and silver arm bracelets and holds a pipe tomahawk. Unsigned and undated watercolor but probably second half of the 18th century. (National Archives of Canada, C108983)

He too was known and respected by many of the chiefs present who must have shared his grief for his slain brother. Would they take up their war tomahawks and join him to take revenge on the English? The meeting ended on this invitation and the chiefs went away to consider the question by themselves. To help their deliberations, a couple of casks of wine were given for them to drink at their feast. A couple of hours later, the chiefs had agreed to take up the war tomahawk and, with the French officers, sang the Indians' war song.

De Villiers seeks the Virginians

On 28 June, at ten in the morning, de Villiers left Fort Duquesne at the head of his force. To his 500 French and Canadians were now added hundreds of Indians – at least 300 according to J.C.B., one of the French soldiers in the contingent – although their number varied and obviously grew along the way. On 29 July a party of "Mississaquin" Indians joined the column and the next day the force reached a shed built by the English where a guard of 20 men was left. De Villiers proceeded swiftly yet cautiously, leaving his dugout canoes and moving on land from 1 July. His main force was preceded by numerous small parties of scouts fanning out in front of it. The next day, some of Villiers' scouts spotted a few Virginians on patrol and even captured a Virginian soldier. From this man, who claimed he was a deserter, de Villiers learned that Washington's men would hold out in a small fort they had built at Great Meadows. Later that day, de Villiers arrived at Gist's settlement. It consisted of several cabins with fences and some tools left behind and had been abandoned by the Virginians. The trails were now getting very difficult to travel on and this was not helped by the rainy weather.

On 3 June, de Villiers marched on; his scouts captured three more Americans and warned that their fort was not very far. The rain continued. The French and Indians came up to Jumonville Glen, the site of the incident, and found four scalped decaying bodies that were given a decent burial. From there, a cautious de Villiers ordered a screen of scouts ahead of his force, which now marched through the woods in three columns, each led by an officer. As they got nearer to Fort Necessity, some scouts reported to de Villiers that they had been spotted by Anglo-American scouts. He immediately ordered his troops to assume the formation "that is most convenient to fighting in the woods" and continued to advance. The French and Indian force was now in the hills overlooking Fort Necessity, whose swivel guns opened fire, while a body of about 50 Anglo-Americans was sighted to the south in battle formation. If it was an attempt to lure de Villiers into an engagement in the open field near the fort, it had no effect on this experienced wilderness commander. Instead, the French and Indians made their terrifying war cries as they advanced under cover; this was enough for the Anglo-American soldiers to turn back into the entrenchment around the fort.

Fort Necessity surrounded

The French and Indians surrounded Fort Necessity and "approached as near as possible" without exposing themselves to enemy fire. The fort, de Villiers noted, was well situated in the meadow but the woods and nearby heights to the north were within musket range.

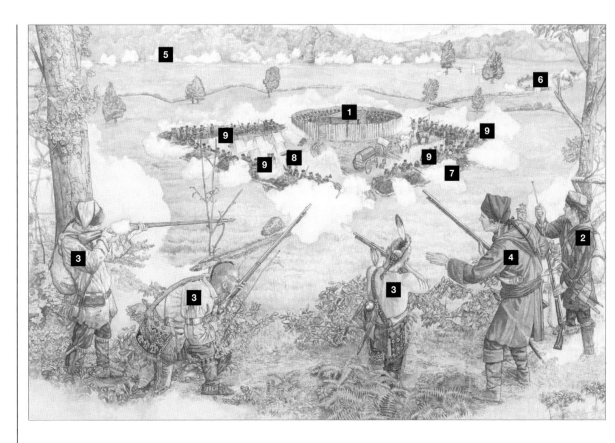

FORT NECESSITY, 3 JULY 1754 (pages 34–35)

Following the Jummonville incident, a strong French and Indian force left Fort Duquesne under the command of Captain Louis Coulon de Villiers seeking Washington and his force. They were soon located at Great Meadows where a small round fort, called Fort Necessity (1), had been built. Villier's men surrounded the fort and, from within the cover of the surrounding woods, opened a brisk fire on the men of the Virginian Provincial and British colonial independent companies defending the fort. The besiegers consisted of a variety of troops, including soldiers of the *Compagnies franches de la Marine* (2). With the exception of their gray-white and blue fatigue caps, their appearance was essentially the same as the Canadian militia, consisting of a capot, mitasses, breechclout or breeches, and moccasins and was usually worn on wilderness campaigns by the French regular colonial soldiers. They were armed with the M1728 .69 caliber musket and had the colonial troops' regulation ventral cartridge box and powder horn. On campaign, bayonets were retained but tomahawks replaced swords. They also carried several knives like the Canadian militiamen and Indians. The Indians (3) were usually armed with the light caliber, but dependable, Tulle trade (or hunting) musket, tomahawks, knives and ball-headed war clubs. Here, their costume and decoration are typical of the northeastern Indian nations at the time. The buckskin pouch carried over their shoulder was invariably highly decorated with beadwork. A Canadian militia officer (4) wears a brown capot, the typical Canadian hooded coat, with a woolen sash, a cap, long leather moccasin-like soft boots, breeches or breechclouts – all items worn almost universally by Canadians in the 18th century. The only indicators of his rank would be his gorget (not visible) and his sword. This group is shown on a small wooded hill overlooking Fort Necessity, but there were troops in the forest all round the fort (5) and even in the small barn and corral (6) seen in the background. For the French and Indians, in good cover, the fort is little more than a shooting gallery. Trenches (7) had been dug giving the fort a roughly square perimeter. The soldiers of the Virginia Regiment and of the British independent companies (8), shown in their red uniforms, tried to reply to the fire of Villiers' force as best they could using their muskets and even a few swivel guns (9) mounted around the perimeter. Their fire proved largely ineffective however and, finding himself in a hopeless situation with casualties mounting, Washington had little choice but to surrender.
(Stephen Walsh)

ABOVE **Grenadiers, 1750s. Halket's 44th Foot (left) and Dunbar's 48th Foot (right). The British troops were issued linen waistcoat and breeches for the 1755 campaign. The two grenadiers companies of the 44th and 48th were the elite of Braddock's army and the French and Indians knew it. Three days before the battle, Braddock had sent grenadiers to deal with a skirmish at the rear of the column, "on whose arrival the Indians fled". Prime targets at the Monongahela, most of the grenadiers were lost. Cecil C.P. Lawson after D. Morrier. (Anne S.K. Brown Military Collection, Brown University, Providence, USA. Author's photo)**

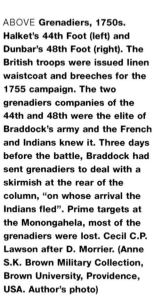

Inside Fort Necessity was George Washington's force of some 400 men. It had swung from confidence to near despair in a few weeks. Initially flushed with optimism following their victory over Jumonville's party at the end of May, the Virginians were much encouraged by the arrival in June of Captain James McKay leading an Independent Company of about 100 soldiers from South Carolina, rushed to Virginia as reinforcements. These were regular British colonial troops and there were soon strains between young Washington, the upstart militia officer with his band of provincials, and McKay with his soldiers. The regulars would not participate in building Washington's road to the Monongahela without extra pay, something that the provincials did as part of their duty. However, Washington was encouraged to receive six swivel guns, which were installed at Fort Necessity.

A more significant worry for both Washington and McKay was the reluctance of the local Indians to join them against the French. By mid-June, the Half-King had gone and few others apart from some Senecas, most of them being women and children, were eager to join the Anglo-American troops at Fort Necessity. Indian nations were just as unstable in their alliances with the British as they were with the French. The news of the Virginians' ambush of Jumonville must have had a sobering effect among the Indians; they knew that Onontio, although far away, would have his men strike back. The wiser course was not to get involved and, as days went by, even the few Indians left at Fort Necessity vanished; a rumor had reached them that a strong force had left Fort Duquesne to avenge Jumonville …

The truth of the rumor was confirmed to soldiers working on road construction some 13 miles (21km) from Fort Necessity. French and Indian scouts appeared in the area and a few men disappeared. Obviously, the place was no longer safe and the soldiers returned to Fort Necessity. When they arrived at the fort on 1 July, conditions were far from ideal in the garrison, with as many as 100 men too sick to continue work to improve its defenses. Within two days, de Villiers' French and Indians had them surrounded; the tables had turned.

De Villiers had no artillery to bombard the fort so his only recourse was for his men to pour musket fire into the Anglo-Americans' position. Well covered by the trees in spite of the rain, the soldiers and the Canadian militiamen in particular opened up such a heavy musketry on the fort and its entrenchments that de Villiers worried that they would soon run out of ammunition. The returning fire from the fort's swivel guns and muskets was largely ineffective. The shooting went on until eight in the evening.

Meanwhile, de Villiers took advice from Captain Le Mercier, an artillery officer, to start building fascines to secure the French and Indian positions should their enemies attempt a sortie. It was imperative to completely seal off Fort Necessity. His force was also very tired, having marched and fought under constant rain. At this time, de Villiers wrote, "the Indians said they would leave us the next morning, and that there was the report that drums and the firing of cannon had been heard in the distance." Faced with the sudden withdrawal of his sometime allies and the possibility of an Anglo-American relief force on the way, the time seemed ripe to open negotiations. Hoping that the Anglo-Americans were in disarray within their fort, de Villiers then decided to call on them to surrender. Some French shouted to the fort's garrison that if they wanted to parlay, they would cease fire. Although "expecting a deceit", the offer was accepted and an Anglo-American officer came out; Captain Le Mercier went out to meet him and offered to grant the honors of war should the garrison surrender, adding that it would otherwise be difficult to control the Indians.

Washington and McKay knew they were doomed. Their fort was being targeted from all sides and there was no hope of escape; well-aimed shots had already left 31 killed and some 70 wounded including 12 Virginian soldiers killed and 43 wounded. Clearly, Fort Necessity and its surrounding trenches did not provide much cover and more men would be mowed down. "The most tremendous rain" was coming down turning the interior of the fort into a morass and setting "everything afloat". The rain "filled our trenches with water [and] wet, not only the ammunition in the Cartouche boxes and the firelocks, but that [ammunition] which was in" the fort. Some of the men, discouraged and afraid, had turned to their bottles of spirits and were said to be drunk.

In spite of all this, Washington declined the French invitation to talk at first but agreed when it was renewed. Then came the problem of languages. Nobody on the French side knew English; in the 18th century

French was the international language that educated gentlemen were expected to know. Washington's French was not up to the task and only Ensign Peyroney and Captain Jacob van Braam knew it relatively well. Washington was not satisfied with the verbal terms and sent Captain van Braam as his interpreter to the French commander to draft a suitable document. Van Braam came back to Washington bearing the surrender documents written in French. In spite of considerable misgivings, Washington and McKay had little choice if they wanted to get out alive and save their men. Some of the clauses were altered and, possibly at Van Braam's insistence, the capitulation was finally signed at about midnight. By then, shooting had stopped for some hours.

The capitulation agreement granted the honors of war, which meant the garrison could evacuate, with drums beating, to Virginia carrying its weapons including a cannon with colors and personal baggage, that hostages would be left for the safe return of the men of Jumonville's party taken prisoner, that this area was the domain of the king of France, that the garrison of Fort Necessity was not to bear arms for a year and that

Drummer, *Compagnies franches de la Marine*, 1750s. Drummers were not usually part of wilderness expeditions but Jumonville's party included one by the name, or nickname, of La Batterie. This strengthens the claim that it was not a war party but an embassy escort. Drummers of the regular colonial troops wore the King's livery of blue turned up with red, decorated with the royal livery lace. Reconstruction by Eugène Lelièpvre. (Parks Canada)

Eastern woodland Indians, mid-18th century. The warrior at left is in summer dress and that at right wears winter clothing. The chief in the center is based on accounts of gifts given by the French to Indian chiefs in the early 1750s. Reconstruction by David Rickman. (Canadian Department of National Defence)

every effort would be made to contain the Indians. The French version of the document contained the word "assassinat" which Van Braam translated as the "death" of Jumonville. Did Washington understand that, in signing the capitulation document, he was admitting to having assassinated Jumonville? The question has never been resolved and probably never will.

Captains Robert Stobo and Van Braam were left with de Villiers as hostages until they could be exchanged. The garrison left Fort Necessity early on the morning of 4 July, even before the French arrived to take possession of it. According to J.C.B., they found the place quite messy with remains of demolished rum and salted meat barrels, 25 wounded or sick men left behind and the unburied bodies of 12 men killed. The Indians had agreed to the capitulation but wanted booty that now escaped them. When they learned that Washington's men had departed, some warriors went after the column of retreating Anglo-Americans and captured ten stragglers, whom they brought back to de Villiers. The French commander chastised the Indians as this was contrary to the capitulation agreement and asked them to return these men. The Indians were upset and killed and scalped three but let the rest go back.[7]

Meanwhile, the French soldiers and Canadian militiamen razed Fort Necessity to the ground and broke the swivel guns left behind. Washington and his troops eventually reached Will's Creek (Fort Cumberland). The proud young lieutenant-colonel must have been humbled and would have felt his career all but finished after presiding over what was, in the short term, a decisive defeat. The French victory had shown that their arms prevailed in the wilderness, secured the Ohio and, just as important, ensured that nearly all Indian nations in the area would side with the French. Yet within a few months Washington's name, if scorned in Versailles, would become internationally famous and he would be hailed as a hero in London.

Governor Dinwiddie reacted to the news of the capitulation with praise for the bravery of Washington and his men who had no chance of success against "900 French & Indians". He squarely laid blame on the considerable delay of the two New York Independent Companies to reach the area; had these additional 160 regulars been there, things might have been different. At first, Dinwiddie felt compelled to respect the terms of the capitulation "in order to recover our two Capts who are hostages" but as time passed, this attitude changed. Once back to the safety of Fort Cumberland and, eventually, Virginia, Washington, McKay and other officers openly proclaimed that they had no intention of respecting the terms of the capitulation they had signed. They interpreted the terms to apply only to the sick men and baggage that had been left behind and had given "no parole for themselves" and stood ready "to proceed with other Forces" against the French. This was without a doubt a highly spurious interpretation of the document they had signed and extremely weak justification for annulling the terms of the capitulation.

By late August, Dinwiddie had the necessary justification to break the terms and accuse the French of cruelty and duplicity. He had now received information that the French and Indians had "acted contrary to the Law of Nat[ion]s in taking our People Prisoners after the

Gunner, Royal Artillery, 1750s. The gunners of Captain Ord's company likely also wore "Osnabrig" linen waistcoats and breeches during the campaign. They had black gaiters for most duties and white gaiters "with black buttons" for parades according to Royal Artillery orders. Reconstruction by Derek FitzJames. (PRO, WO 55/640). (Parks Canada)

The cabin that was used by George Washington at Will's Creek (later Fort Cumberland) in 1754 still stands in a park on the site of the fort which is now in the city of Cumberland, Maryland. (Author's photo)

Capitulat[io]n agreed upon, offering [th]em to Sale, and at last missing of the Sale, sending them Prisoners to Canada, an unprecedented, unjust and barbarous Usage; they pretended they were Prison[e]rs to the Ind[ian]s; the same reason subsists in regard to our Prisoners, the Half King insisting on their being his." In short, while the French prisoners were safely kept in Virginia, the French had abandoned some of the Anglo-Americans to the Indians. Thus, the unwarranted capture of a few departing Anglo-American soldiers by French-allied Indians provided the pretext to render the terms of the capitulation null and void.

A month earlier, Governor General Duquesne, no doubt sensing the opportunity given to the Anglo-Americans to break the terms, had instructed Commandant de Contrecoeur to inform the Indians that it was his personal order to release the prisoners they had brought to Fort Duquesne. By early September, Duquesne's mood had changed for the Baron de Longueuil, acting as chief of staff, had brought him a capital document just arrived from the Ohio: a translation of Washington's journal that had been seized by Villiers' men at Fort Necessity. Duquesne found it a "priceless document" revealing the putridity "of the English" and of the Iroquois Indians but that, in the event, the English had been duped because their Indians had vanished when de Villiers' force had arrived on the scene. The governor general concluded that there could be "nothing more undignified and low and even darker than the feelings and the way of thinking of this Washington".

The royal courts and ministers of both France and England were outraged; there had been other incidents, notably in India, but this was much more serious. The French were convinced Jumonville had been assassinated – murdered – while the British would have none of it. Both sides were mobilizing troops and, in the spring of 1755, battalions were embarking for North America.

Jumonville Glen, Pennsylvania. This is the high spot in the forest looking down from the cliff where Washington and his men spied on the French encamped below on 27 May 1754. The ensuing action in which Jumonville and many of his men were killed was the effective start of the war in North America. (Author's photo)

The lower ground at Jumonville Glen where the ensign and his party were encamped when they were ambushed on 27 May 1754. (Author's photo)

THE STORM CLOUDS GATHER

The most ambitious military plans for the campaign of 1755 were formed in Great Britain in the fall of 1754. By October 1754, although war was not officially declared, Colonel Halket's 44th and Colonel Dunbar's 48th regiments, each having 700 rank and file, with a train of artillery "consisting of six light six pounders, four light twelve pounders & four Howitzers ... with a full proportion of ammunition and store for the same" were ordered to go to Virginia and capture Fort Duquesne; a provincial army would take Fort Saint-Frédéric (Crown Point, NY) while two new regular regiments, the 50th and the 51st, would be raised to 1,000 men each in New York and New England by colonels Shirley and Pepperell. There were three regular regiments already in Nova Scotia, Colonel Hopson's 40th, Colonel Warburton's 45th and Colonel Lascelles'

ABOVE **Washington's Virginians and the Half-King's Indians firing on Jumonville and his men. US National Park Service. From an interpretation plaque at the site. (Author's photo)**

RIGHT **The site of Fort Duquesne, just behind the fountain at the head of the Allegheny and Monongahela rivers, where the news of Jumonville's death was received and from where, a few days later, a sizeable force under Captain Louis Coulon de Villiers set out to find Washington and his Virginians. (Author's photo)**

47th with a company of Royal Artillery and Captain Goreham's company of Rangers. With the assistance of some Massachusetts provincial troops sent to Nova Scotia, they would take forts Beauséjour and Gaspareau. In January 1755, the establishment of British regiments in North America was raised from 700 to 1,000 men each, the new men to be recruited in the American colonies. Furthermore, the Royal Navy was to prevent French reinforcements from reaching Canada.

The French too had their plans. The reinforcement of New France was the priority and six battalions would be sent, four to Québec and two to Louisbourg. The battalions at Québec would, under General the Baron de Dieskau, secure Lake George and take Fort William Henry. The battalions left Brest in May. On 16 June 1755, Admiral Boscawen's Royal Navy squadron tried to intercept the French convoy off Newfoundland but, except for two ships, the French continued their voyage safely. The battle nevertheless confirmed the undeclared state of war between France and Britain. The official declaration of hostilities was finally made a year later.

The two British regiments with a train of artillery had left Britain earlier. They sailed for America in January 1755 and landed in Virginia in March. Major-General Edward Braddock led these troops and was commander-in-chief of all troops, provincial or regular.

Braddock's preparations

The general and the staff officers of an army setting out to capture Fort Duquesne faced many difficulties, and of a type not usually encountered by an army campaigning in Europe. Perhaps the first and possibly the most significant problem was the lack of any reliable detailed maps of the country they must traverse. This was not helped by the fact that, west of Fort Cumberland, the country was a near total wilderness of mountains and forests. There might be trails of a sort, but there was no road worthy of the name; yet Braddock's army would have a considerable number of wagons. Unlike an army campaigning in Europe, Braddock's force would have to transport all its food with it. In the frontier's wilderness, there was no possibility of purchasing (or seizing) food from towns along the way. As a result Braddock would probably require many more wagons than a corresponding force campaigning in Europe.

Even water might present a problem; ideally, in North America, the army would move by river, with ample water available for drinking, cooking and washing. A river could also be used for transporting the army and its supplies. Although the Anglo-American army would initially move along the Potomac River as far as Will's Creek where Fort Cumberland was built, the Potomac then turned southwest. The army had to march on towards the northwest to reach Fort Duquesne and there was no major waterway until one reached the Monongahela River some 75 miles away. The Monongahela presented further difficulties as it flowed from the south until it turned west only a dozen miles or so east of the fort. It was a meandering river, full of twists and turns, shallow in some places and with rapids at others. Following the course of the river might well take longer than marching cross-country. Another smaller river, the Youghiogheny, flowed northwest from present-day Maryland until it reached the Monongahela River about a dozen miles east of Fort Duquesne, but the Youghiogheny was even more tortuous than the Monongahela and hardly a viable option. There was thus no practicable

Captain François Coulon de Villiers, like his brother Louis Coulon de Villiers, swore revenge for the killing of Jumonville for he was another elder brother serving in the colonial *Compagnies franches de la Marine*. From 1756 to 1759, he participated in several celebrated actions including the routing of Highlanders as they approached Fort Duquesne in 1758. Captured near Fort Niagara and exchanged, he went to Louisiana where he joined the Spanish service as commandant of Natchitoches, prospered and later became an *Alcade* of New Orleans. (Print after a portrait made later in life.)

Fort Necessity with some of its entrenchments seen from above. (National Park Service.)

waterway between the Potomac and the Monongahela almost as far as its junction with the Allegheny.

The difficulties were not insurmountable. Although General Braddock and his staff officers could not rely on dependable maps, the country to be crossed had seen many visitors previously and was not unknown. Scouts could be depended upon to provide reliable information, as would Lieutenant-Colonel Washington, formerly a surveyor, who had certainly become familiar with the area in the previous couple of years. It was obvious to all that crossing the wilderness by land was the best course. As for a road, the existing trails going west would simply have to be improved wherever needed to allow passage of the army with its artillery and supply wagons. It presented a logistical challenge to General Braddock, but a challenge that could easily be met by enlisting American provincial companies as carpenters more than as front line fighting troops. More American companies would be enlisted as rangers and light horse to provide advance warning in the forest. A detachment of sailors would also be brought along to deal with the navigation of the Allegheny, Monongahela and Ohio rivers once Fort Duquesne was invested. Taking a sizeable army across a substantial wilderness to reach its objective was undoubtedly no ordinary challenge, but General Braddock and his staff had the resources and the manpower to carry it out. Their planning was equal to the task and they had every reason to be confident as they assembled at Fort Cumberland at the end of May 1755.

In the French camp

For the French, their geostrategic situation in the Ohio was very different from that of the Anglo-Americans. New France's basic strategy rested on control of the main rivers for transport and communications. Although a long way from their main base at Montréal, the French and Canadians could carry impressive quantities of supplies, arms and men far into the wilderness with relative ease. Great canoe brigades assembled at Lachine west of Montréal and traveled along the rivers and lakes, punctuated by occasional portages, to their destination: a fort in the middle of the wilderness. From that wilderness base, they would venture in smaller parties along smaller waterways and eventually leave their canoes and continue on foot, as they had done to invest Washington and his force at Fort Necessity.

In this regard, the measures taken by Captain de Beaujeu in the spring of 1755 were typical of the flexibility of the French system of communication and supply across a 500-mile (804km) route. De Beaujeu had left Montréal on 20 April to relieve Captain de Contrecoeur as commandant of the Ohio at Fort Duquesne. Arriving at Fort Presqu'Isle in early June, he received a dispatch from de Contrecoeur written on 18 May stating that the Anglo-Americans had a large army of some 3,000

Fort Necessity was built by Washington and his men in June 1754 "out of Necessity" as the strong force of French and Indians led by Captain de Villiers, Jumonville's half-brother, caught up with them. It was a very simple, small, round stockade fort with trenches outside. This reconstruction was made on the original site by the US National Parks Service near the actual site at Farmington, Pennsylvania. (Author's photo)

Fort Necessity as seen from the side of its gate. Note the swivel gun in the foreground. (Author's photo)

men from England that had arrived in Virginia and they were about to invade the Ohio according to several Anglo-American soldiers that had deserted from the advanced British camp at Will's Creek. Instantly perceiving the urgency of the threat, de Beaujeu stayed some days at Presqu'Isle sending out a series of orders to Fort Niagara for reinforcements, arms and supplies, tons of which were soon on their way to Fort Presqu'Isle in 13 boats.

An idea of the length of time such a trek could take is given by Canonnier-Bombardier Bonin who was part of a force of 600 regulars and militia sent to the Ohio in early 1755. They left Montréal on 17 February, traveling with sleds and on snowshoes along the upper St Lawrence River to Lake Ontario and reached Fort Frontenac on 5 March. There they boarded vessels that reached Fort Niagara ten days later and, crossing the Niagara peninsula, they boarded boats at Lake Erie and reached Fort

ABOVE **Fort Necessity as the French and Indians would have seen it from in the woods of the nearby hill. This vantage point offered the French and Indians a good view of any attempts to break out and the occasional target moving within the fort. (Author's photo)**

RIGHT **Fort Necessity was very small and its only dwelling was a small wooden hut as shown in this reconstruction on the site of the original fort. (Author's photo)**

Presqu'Isle on 27 March. Leaving 300 men there, the rest of the party marched to Fort Le Bœuf where they boarded bark and dugout canoes. They made fast time down French Creek and the Allegheny River, reaching Fort Duquesne on 8 April, some 50 days after their departure from Montréal. A courier would be faster: a dispatch written at Fort Duquesne on 23 January 1755 was received 39 days later at Montréal on 5 March.

Rather than moving immediately to Fort Duquesne, de Beaujeu spent more time at forts Presqu'Isle and Le Bœuf to requisition all the supplies and manpower available. As the new commandant of Fort Duquesne, he was the senior officer and had the authority to do this. He also received more dispatches from Commandant de Contrecoeur at Fort Duquesne encouraging him to bring all he could to the fort as well as providing news of the British army. On 8 June, de Contrecoeur wrote to de Beaujeu that a British deserter had brought the news that the Anglo-American army was on the march. Following this intelligence, de Contrecoeur sent out a party of some 60 Indians with 11 cadets of the *Compagnies franches de la Marine* to harass the British column. De Beaujeu finally reached Fort Duquesne at the end of June.

By the time de Contrecoeur greeted the officer who was to relieve him at Fort Duquesne, much had changed since the Governor General had signed that order himself in February. The effects of the previous year's incident that took Jumonville's life had come full circle. War between France and Britain had still not been declared but news had reached Fort Duquesne that the British were not the only ones dispatching troops to North America; France was sending an even more powerful force: six army battalions were on their way to Louisbourg and Canada under an army general, the German-born Baron de Dieskau. Reinforcements for the colonial troops were also expected and the Marquis de Vaudreuil, the Canadian-born son of a former governor general of New France, veteran colonial officer and previously governor of Louisiana, was to relieve Governor General Duquesne. However, to the officers and men at Fort Duquesne, as good as all this might sound, it was of little comfort as none of these troops would ever reach them in time to confront the British forces marching towards the forks of the Ohio River.

Washington's garrison of Virginians try to resist the French and Indians in early July 1754. Print after H.A. Ogden.

Nevertheless the French still had one major "trump card", which they played to full effect. The call had gone out to all *Compagnies franches de la Marine* officers in wilderness outposts and forts of the Great Lakes to rally all the friendly Indians they could and have them come down to Fort Duquesne. The English and the scorned American long knives were marching to vanquish the French. If the redcoats won that battle, it was really the Indians that would lose the most for the Anglo-Americans would chase them away from their hunting grounds forever. The French and Canadians would fight them every inch of the way but would not the children of Onontio fight as well? As the days of June came and went, more and more canoes filled with warriors arrived at Fort Duquesne's landing. Already, on 16 June, Commandant de Contrecoeur had met with the Ottawas, the Potawatamies that had come from Michigan, the Senecas, the Shawnees and the Delawares to reassure them that, like the wing of the bird that protects its young, the French would never abandon their children to the English and that Onontio had raised his tomahawk for them to join. His words were no doubt well received. Some of the most influential chiefs were gathering at Fort Duquesne: Pucksinwah, Athanese, White Eyes and Pontiac. And from Michili-mackinac, the young man who was both an Indian chief and a French officer: Ensign Charles-Michel de Langlade who, in spite of his youth, could influence the Indians to act in unison thanks to his unique background and exceptional talent. To lead them now came Captain de Beaujeu, an officer of legendary fame in New France, famous for the brilliant part he had played in the triumphant raid on Grand Pré (Nova Scotia) eight years earlier and greatly respected by the Indians as a result of his postings on the frontier. Desperate as the situation may have seemed to the French and Indians and heavy as the odds stacked against them undoubtedly were, capitulating was never considered for a moment. Even the idea of blowing up Fort Duquesne and evacuating was quickly forgotten. On the contrary, the French and Indians were determined to give the enemy a fight he would remember.

BRADDOCK MOVES WEST

On 30 May, the assembled British and American army at Fort Cumberland was ready to move west into the wilderness. The army was divided into two brigades as follows:

First Brigade: Colonel Sir Peter Halket:
Halket's 44th Foot
Captain Rutherford's New York Independent Company
Captain Polson's Virginia Provincial Artificers (or Carpenters)
Captain Peronnee's Virginia Provincial Rangers
Captain Wagner's Virginia Provincial Rangers
Captain Dagworthy's Maryland Provincial Rangers

Second Brigade: Colonel Thomas Dunbar:
Dunbar's 48th Foot
Captain Demeries' South Carolina Independent Companies' detachments
Captain Dobb's North Carolina Provincial Rangers
Captain Mercer's Virginia Provincial Artificers (or Carpenters)
Captain Steven's Virginia Provincial Rangers
Captain Hogg's Virginia Provincial Rangers
Captain Cox's Virginia Provincial Rangers

The detachment of Royal Navy seamen was to encamp with the Second Brigade, Stewart's troop of light horse was separate from the brigades, and Ord's detachment of Royal Artillery would be with the guns and the train.

With the 1,600 or so British and American officers and men, there were hundreds of wagoners and camp followers. The number of wagons with teams of horses stood at about 200. Of these, some 146 were furnished by the colony of Pennsylvania. Colonial supplies for the expedition had been difficult to obtain and the cause of some delay in setting out. The remaining rolling stock consisted mostly of British Army tumbrels and wagons of various sorts. It is uncertain if guns and limbers were part of the total number of wagons. In any event, the train of artillery with Braddock's army consisted of:

Six brass 6-pdr cannons
Four brass 12-pdr cannons
Four 8in. brass howitzers
15 4$\frac{2}{5}$in. brass Coehorn mortars

There were hundreds of horses – at least 800 – needed to pull the wagons and the artillery: each wagon required four horses, each 12-pdr cannon five horses and no less than seven of the strongest horses were needed to move one howitzer. There were also 510 pack horses provided by Pennsylvania; packhorse being a much easier means of transporting

British army 6-pdr field gun on a traveling carriage. Of the cannons brought over for the expedition, the 6-pdrs were the only ones to make it to the Monongahela battlefield, the others being too heavy to travel in the wilderness. Although bravely served by the gunners, they proved almost useless against the largely unseen enemy in the forest and were all captured by the French and Indians. Reproduction at Fort Ligonier. (Author's photo)

British army mortar on a flat wagon. Braddock's artillery included 15 relatively light Coehorn mortars, such as shown, mounted on mortar beds. For traveling, the beds would be mounted on a flat truck-carriage. Reproduction at Fort Ligonier. (Author's photo)

supplies on wilderness trails. The number of non-combatants such as wagoners devoted to the transport of the army's supplies would have been at least 300 and probably more. The number of dependents, sutlers and other camp followers must have varied even as the army was marching but must have been at least 100–200 persons of both sexes and would have included some children.

So, as it started from Fort Cumberland into the wilderness, Braddock's army would have included at least 2,000 people and over 900 horses.

RIGHT **British army powder cart. These were absolutely essential to any train of artillery. This reproduction, as with the other carriages and carts illustrated, was made according to the specifications in John Muller's Treatise of Artillery first published in 1757. Reproduction at Fort Ligonier. (Author's photo)**

BELOW **British army wagon of the mid-18th century. This type of army wagon proved too heavy for wilderness trails and American horses. General Braddock had them sent back to Fort Cumberland on 11 June 1755. Reproduction at Fort Ligonier. (Author's photo)**

On 29 May, a strong vanguard of 600 men under Major Russell Chapman with 50 wagons loaded with supplies left Fort Cumberland heading west. Sir John St Clair, two engineers, Royal Navy Lt Spendelow, several sailors and Indians accompanied Chapman's force. The vanguard's purpose was to find a way through the mountains and clear a road 12 feet (3.66m) wide to Little Meadows some 20 miles (32km) away. The construction of the road was a formidable enough task for the soldiers of the army, but getting over Will's Mountain just west of Fort Cumberland proved to be even more challenging. Three wagons were totally wrecked and many damaged in the process. The following day,

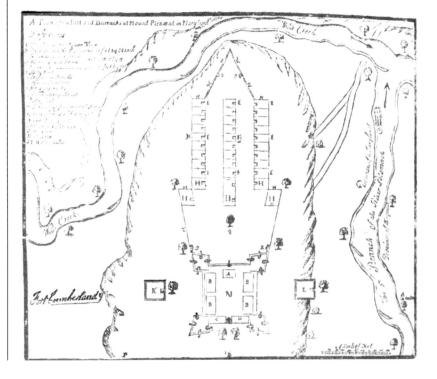

Fort Cumberland, the former Will's Creek fort until renamed in honor of the Duke of Cumberland by General Braddock in 1755. Print of a period plan after Lowdermilk's *History of Cumberland, Maryland*.

During the 1755 campaign, Captain Jack, who led volunteer woodsmen in western Pennsylvania, tried to warn General Braddock about the tactics of the French and Indians. George Washington, who was then Braddock's colonial ADC concurred but all this made little impression on the British general. Print after H. Ogden.

General Braddock himself came up to see what was blocking Chapman's way. Appraised of the situation, he decided to detach 300 more men to Chapman, two thirds of the troops to be employed as pioneers. Just then, luck smiled on the army; Lt Spendelow arrived with the good news that the sailors had found a pass that went through a valley around the mountain. General Braddock ordered a survey that confirmed the discover; the road through the pass was built in less than three days, and the army pressed on.

The road built by the army as it moved west closely followed the Nemacolin Indian trail; it went as far as present day Jumonville, Pennsylvania, a little further than Great Meadows where Fort Necessity had stood. Christopher Gist had been the army's chief guide since 27 May so it is possible he suggested this route. Washington and his men had used it the previous year and it was natural that Sir John St Clair's vanguard should use it as the basis of the army's road. It has been suggested that, with hindsight, a better way might have been found, but there seems to have been no knowledge of another practicable route in 1755. Indeed, Colonel Washington, who had arrived at Fort Cumberland to join General Braddock as his American aide-de-camp on 30 May, seems to have concurred with the choice. As for General Braddock, he was getting acquainted with the wilderness, which, so far, was not causing overwhelming difficulties.

But difficulties there were, and none of them caused by the French and Indians. The mountainous nature of the country at the outset of the march and the irregular topography of the whole area as well as the generally wooded character of the countryside made the building of a road a very tough job. The road built by the troops as well as the lighter American draught horses increasingly imposed their limits. For the next ten days, animals and men toiled constantly, moving the heaviest pieces of artillery and somehow coping with the 16 heavy army wagons that had

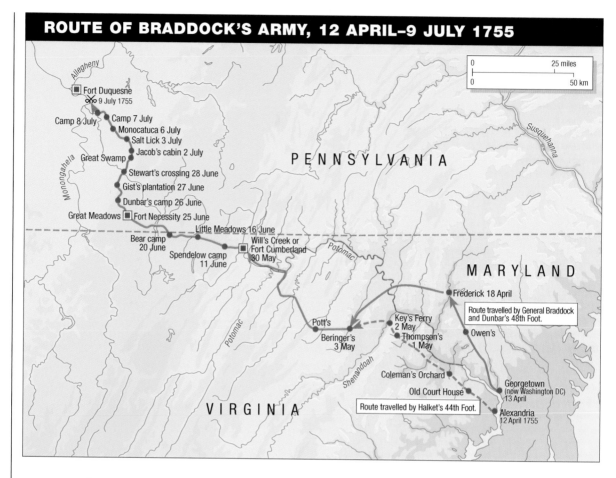

come over from England with the British troops. The lighter American horses simply could not pull these wagons over such a road without constant help from the men themselves. The American horses were of lighter breeds than the heavy English draught horses that should have come along with the army's artillery train and supply wagons; to have the American horses pull such inordinate weights over a rough road in the wilderness was simply to exhaust them and their teamsters. The rough wilderness road itself could not take the immense weight of the artillery for long, nor could it support the army's heavy wagons. As a result, the army's progress seemed painfully slow to General Braddock and his officers, as little as two miles (3.2km) a day, with little prospect of improving.

On 11 June, the army had progressed only as far as Spendelow Camp, about 25 miles (40km), and thus was still in Maryland. On that day, General Braddock called a council of his officers to resolve the problem. As Lieutenant Orme reported it, the general told them that; "it would be impossible to continue the March without some alternations, which he was convinced they would really assist in, as they had hitherto expressed the greatest spirit and inclination for the service. He recommended to them to send back to Fort Cumberland all such baggage as was not absolutely necessary" and also asked them to contribute any private horse they could spare to the army's transport. This had an excellent effect on the officers and most of them sent back the excess baggage, contributed about 100 horses "and made use of Soldiers tents the rest of

View of the Monongahela River looking east taken in April 2003. In July 1755, Braddock's army crossed its second ford in the area of the weir to the right. The field of battle was inland to the left and is now obliterated by modern buildings. (Author's photo)

the Campaign". It was also decided to send back to Fort Cumberland two of the 6-pdr cannons, four Coehorn mortars and some of the ordnance stores with an escort of some 50 "of the worst men" from the Independent companies and the American rangers. Another 50 men were dispatched to escort workmen and 28 of the soldiers' wives were sent to Philadelphia. The 16 very heavy army wagons were also ordered to return; their content was unloaded into ordinary farm wagons.

Skirmishes in the forest

Thus "lightened" the march continued, with the often twisting narrow trail being transformed into a narrow road over the coming days. The terrain was rugged with hills and creeks to cross, and on each side of the road a silent and seemingly impenetrable forest of tall pines and dark foliage bore down on the column of troops. There should have been scouts on either flank but, more often than not, the woods proved almost impossible to traverse and the flank guards feared becoming isolated so that almost everyone was on the road. The formation of Braddock's army was thus reduced to a winding narrow column of mixed wagons, horses, teamsters and soldiers that might stretch some four miles (6.4km). This certainly left it exposed to possible raids and hit-and-run attacks but the Anglo-American troops felt they were too far away from Fort Duquesne to be at serious risk.

Somewhat awed by the immense trees towering high over them, many in the column also felt they were being watched; they were right! The French officers at Fort Duquesne were frequently receiving information from allied Indians as to the progress of the army. They also knew from many previous scouting forays that the terrain was difficult for such a force to cross. Their scouts simply observed the column from a safe distance and were rarely if ever seen. Many "suspect" sightings by the Anglo-Americans were dismissed as simply an animal moving in the forest, but occasionally and unseen French and Indian scouts were also out there. Commandant de Contrecoeur had known from four scouts that Major Chapman's vanguard had preceded General Braddock's

The field of the battle of the Monongahela, site of Braddock's defeat, as seen in the mid-19th century, about 100 years after the battle. The forest that covered the area at the time of the battle has been mostly cleared and a few houses dot the landscape but the area is otherwise much as it would have been in 1755. This view was taken from the south side of the Monongahela River, which can be seen in the middle of the picture. Print after Paul Weber.

army marching out of Fort Cumberland and its strength was estimated at 700 men, which was an amazingly close reckoning. This information was supplemented some days later by reports from a British deserter and Abenaki Indian scouts that the marching army was approaching the site of Fort Necessity with 14–15 guns and about 3,000 men. De Contrecoeur sent out several more parties to observe and, if possible, to harass the column. Although no blood was yet shed, the Anglo-Americans were growing apprehensive. Captain Chomley's servant wrote as early as 13 June that "We Expect the French Indians to attack us Every day."[8]

The Anglo-American army was nevertheless slowly marching west. The road remained very rugged and rocky and even the lighter wagons were proving unsuitable. On 16 July, the First Brigade reached Little Meadows where the army would regroup at the stockaded camp erected there. A new development that passed largely unnoted was a brief skirmish with lurking "French" Indians noted by Chomley's servant. The army's progress was still considered much too slow by General Braddock. He instructed more soldiers' wives to go back to Fort Cumberland, left as many wagons behind as he could and had officers' baggage reduced yet further; Washington's was down to a single portmanteau. Sir John St Clair had also received information from an Indian who claimed to have left Fort Duquesne on 8 July that its garrison was no more than 100 French and 70 Indians. Such a low figure was hardly believable but was encouraging; General Braddock probably did not believe these numbers but the garrison was certainly much weaker than his army. It increased his determination to get to the fort faster, before French reinforcements could arrive from Canada.

Braddock presses ahead

The only way to increase the speed of the march was to split up the army, a calculated risk. General Braddock called an officers' council at which it was decided to leave some of the artillery, including two 6-pdr cannons with accompanying gunners, some of the Virginia troops, the cumbersome and slow supply wagons with most wagoners, and other

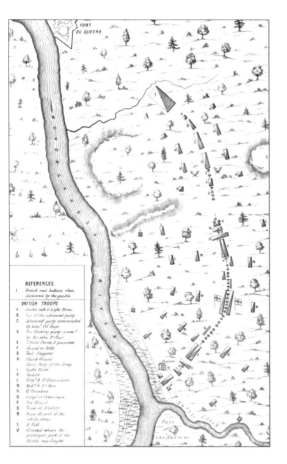

REFERENCES.

French and Indians when discovered by the guides

BRITISH TROOPS

A Guides with 6 Light Horse
B Van of the advanced party
C Advanced party commanded by Lieut. Col. Gage
D The Working party commanded by Sir John St Clair
E 2 Field Pieces & 6 pounders
F Guard to Ditto
G Tool Waggons
H Main Body of the Army
I Light Horse
K Sailors
L Serjt & 20 Grenadiers
M Rob.t & 2d Men
N 12 Pounders
O Comp.al demandeurs
P Tin Guard
Q Train of Artillery
R Rear Guard of the whole Army
A A Hill
V Ground where the principal part of the Battle was fought

Plan of the British and American army as it encounters the French and Indian force (No. 1). Although based on a contemporary source and much reproduced in 19th and 20th century histories, many details do not agree with accounts of the battle and it should be used with caution. For instance, Stewart's Light Horse is shown mostly on the left flank near the river.

non-combatants at Little Meadows under the command of Colonel Dunbar who was to regroup the supply train.

General Braddock's scheme was "for a Detachment of About twelve hundred of the best Troops" to march ahead faster. The troops forging ahead with General Braddock were the 44th and 48th regiments, the New York Independent Company, three companies of Virginia rangers, a company of Virginia artificers/carpenters, Stewart's Virginia light horse, the detachment of seamen and some gunners. The actual number of men with General Braddock came to more than 1,200. Hamilton mentioned 1,373 and Mackellar 1,469 all ranks present at the battle that would soon take place. Colonel Dunbar and the remainder of the army would follow later with the additional guns, ammunition, provisions, wagons and packhorses. This way, General Braddock reasoned, he could rapidly cut off Fort Duquesne before it was reinforced and Colonel Dunbar would join him with additional artillery, the remaining troops and all the necessary supplies during its siege.

On 18 June, Sir John St Clair with Lieutenant-Colonel Gage left with a 400-man vanguard to scout a route. The following day, General Braddock went on with Sir Peter Halket (acting as brigadier) and about 800 men including the two grenadier companies of the 44th and 48th, 500 soldiers, gunners, the detachment of seamen and 18 of Stewart's Light Horse. The train now consisted of four 12-pdr cannons, two 6-pdr cannons, four 8in. howitzers, three Coehorn mortars, 13 artillery wagons and 17 ammunition wagons. Each howitzer was pulled by nine horses, each gun by seven and the wagons by six horses to speed up the march. Packhorses carried provisions for 35 days, all other wagons being left behind.

The march started rather inauspiciously. The British-allied Indians under Chief Monocatuca were ordered to act as scouts for the advance party, but Monocatuca was soon ambushed and captured "by some French and Indians". He was left tied to a tree and soon released as troops came up; but the incident confirmed the enemy to be lurking, well hidden and possibly more numerous and more adept at forest warfare than the few Indians allied to the British. It might have just been an unlucky brush, however, and in any event was certainly no reason to halt. On the column went, not much faster as it took five days to get to Great Crossings, a distance of about 17 miles or less than three and a half miles (5.6km) a day. The road was rough and hilly; block and tackle was sometimes needed to help the artillery and wagons up and down slopes, and when not dealing with rocks and hills the men sometimes found themselves knee deep in a sticky mud. Nevertheless, the army pressed on slowly getting closer to its target. On the 21st, it crossed the modern-day border from Maryland into Pennsylvania. By 24/25 June, it was turning north past Great Meadows and the site of Fort Necessity, approaching Gist's abandoned settlement.

There were now almost daily incidents with lurking French and Indians. De Contrecoeur's men were looking out for anyone who might wander just a little too far from the column. On 24 June alone, a wagoner was wounded and four others fetching horses were killed and scalped. The next day, Lieutenant Orme noted an all too typical incident: "We this day saw several Indians in the woods; the General sent the light horse, our Indians, and some volunteers, to endeavor to surround them, but they returned without seeing them." Progress was nervous and difficult but the army was advancing. Colonel Dunbar with his detachment was also moving on further at the rear. June turned into July by which time the progress of the army had increased a little: on 2 July it covered six miles (9.7km) before it stopped for the night at Jacob's Cabin.

Nearing Fort Duquesne

A decision had to be taken as to what to do next. Sir John St Clair had suggested halting where they were and sending all the horses to speed the progress of Dunbar's detachment. On 3 July, General Braddock called a council of war to consider the issue. It would take as much as 11 days for Dunbar to reach Jacob's Cabin, and the provisions they carried would be "near expended" by waiting that long. As it was also vital to reach Fort Duquesne before French reinforcements arrived, it was decided to press on.

Incidence of French and Indian harassment had been fewer for the last few days. General Braddock was anxious to have his allied Indians "go toward the fort for intelligence" especially as they had declined to scout for the last eight or nine days. He tried again with promises and presents, but to no avail; they would not go out. Thus, the Anglo-American army was practically blind; only Washington, Gist and a few others had been in the area before. The next day, Gist did go out with a couple of Indians; they returned on 6 July with "a French officer's scalp" and word that they had seen "very few men" at the fort, had seen no one between the column and Fort Duquesne and believed very few French and Indian raiders and scouts were out. The officer's scalp story is dubious as the French did not report losing any officer while Gist had narrowly escaped when set upon by two French Indians. As for the absence of lurking enemies, it was an illusion; they showed up raiding the baggage later that very morning causing quite an alarm with nervous soldiers firing at anything that moved; unfortunately, their "friendly fire" killed the son of Chief Monocatuca, a devastating blow to relations with the allied Indians even if he was given a military funeral with a guard of honor firing over his grave.

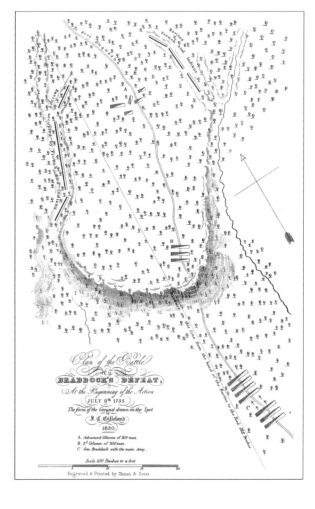

Plan of the battlefield at the beginning of the action from notes "drawn on the spot" by J.C. Gilleland in 1830. It shows the French and Indians already deployed on the flanks, which at this stage they were not, and the hill on the right mentioned in several accounts is not shown.

THE MONONGAHELA, MORNING OF 9 JULY 1755

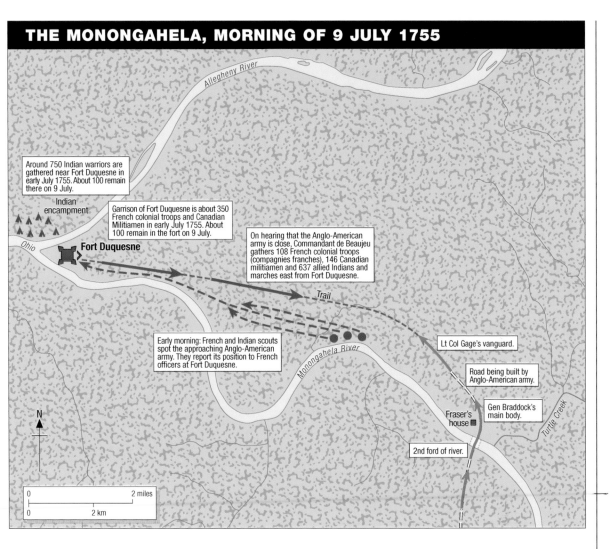

Around 750 Indian warriors are gathered near Fort Duquesne in early July 1755. About 100 remain there on 9 July.

Indian encampment

Garrison of Fort Duquesne is about 350 French colonial troops and Canadian Militiamen in early July 1755. About 100 remain in the fort on 9 July.

On hearing that the Anglo-American army is close, Commandant de Beaujeu gathers 108 French colonial troops (compagnies franches), 146 Canadian militiamen and 637 allied Indians and marches east from Fort Duquesne.

Fort Duquesne

Ohio

Allegheny River

Trail

Monongahela River

Early morning: French and Indian scouts spot the approaching Anglo-American army. They report its position to French officers at Fort Duquesne.

Lt Col Gage's vanguard.

Road being built by Anglo-American army.

Fraser's house

Gen Braddock's main body.

Turtle Creek

2nd ford of river.

N

| 0 | 2 miles |
| 0 | 2 km |

The important thing was to press on now that the objective was near. On 7 July, the army reached Turtle Creek, but proceeding straight to the fort was risky as the terrain ahead was difficult and dangerous. General Braddock thus opted to cross to the west bank of the Monongahela, turn north and then, as the river bent westward, cross it again to the north bank as he neared Fort Duquesne. Scouts had already found suitable fords with gently sloped banks. Once on the north bank of the Monongahela, the Anglo-American army would be only about eight miles (12.9km) from its objective. There was no time to lose and the army set out at once since General Braddock hoped to invest Fort Duquesne by 10 July. Sir Peter Halket worried that the army was advancing almost blind. Sending in scouts before approaching the fort would be wiser, but time was of the essence. Lieutenant-Colonel Gage was sent ahead with a group of chosen men to secure the crossings and ground ahead. By early on 9 July, the ground had been secured and St Clair's workmen began constructing the road. At 6.00am, the army crossed the first ford and at 11.00am the second ford. It re-formed its column and continued its march into the forest. Fort Duquesne was now tantalizingly close.

59

The north-northeast view of the US Steel plant at Braddock, Pennsylvania, seen from the south side of the Monongahela River. As can be appreciated, the heavy industries built since the late 19th century have totally covered what was, in 1755, a forest area with a narrow trail. Note also how the Monongahela has been canalized. Hardly a tree has survived until one reaches the foot of the hills in the distance. (Author's photo)

Meanwhile, in the fort itself de Contrecoeur, de Beaujeu and the other officers were pondering the daily reports of the progress of the Anglo-American army. It was obvious that, despite the natural obstacles and lurking Indians, the enemy was determined to reach and capture the fort. On 7 July, a war council of officers was called to consider what to do. There were really only two options for the French: blow up the fort and retreat, or put up a fight. The officers quickly dismissed the idea of destroying the fort and leaving; there was only one honorable option and that was to confront their enemies.

A general engagement might have been brought on earlier but its outcome would have been risky and these experienced frontier officers had dismissed this option. Apart from the logistical problems over a longer distance, their more numerous enemies might have detected a large party. A failure would, furthermore, have discouraged many allied Indians, and Indians were crucial to French success.

The situation now was different. As General Braddock's army was closing in, all available men were being mustered and, even more important, the Indians were expected to join in. They could see for themselves, that, if they did not assist the French against the Redcoats and the Americans, their own way of life would be threatened and their territories opened to English colonists. The French officers knew that Fort Duquesne was indefensible against an army with artillery; the only option was to ambush and attack it while on the march. Captain Dumas proposed this idea seconded by Captain Courtemanche, and the decision to attack was taken. The French plan was simple: Commandant de Contrecoeur would remain at the fort with a small garrison while Commandant de Beaujeu led a mixed attack force. A force of regulars and militiamen was put together: 108 officers, cadets and enlisted men of the *Compagnies franches de la Marine* assisted by 146 Canadian militiamen for a total of 254 French regulars and Canadian militiamen. With them were about 650 Indians with their chiefs. De Beaujeu had initially wanted to attack Braddock's army at the second ford of the Monongahela but it appears the Indians were somewhat reluctant to do this. It would seem that they preferred, possibly at Ensign de Langlade's suggestion, to ambush the Anglo-American column from both sides once contact had been made. Finally, on 9 July, de Beaujeu, with some 900 French and Indians, left Fort Duquesne at 8.00am and headed east into the forest.

THE BATTLE

The Anglo-American army had crossed the second ford of the Monongahela River "Colours flying, Drums beating and Fifes playing" and marched inland to an abandoned house that had belonged to a trader named Frazer (or Fraser or Frazier). Washington remembered it well as he had rested there on his way back from Fort Le Bœuf a year and a half earlier. From there the army marched west.

At the forefront were some scouts and six troopers of Stewart's light horse, then the vanguard of the advanced party, the advanced party itself under Lieutenant-Colonel Gage, a working party under Sir John St Clair followed by gunners with two 6-pdr cannons, artillery carts and ammunition wagons and the rearguard of the advance party.

Next came Stewart's light horse, sailors, artificers and gunners with three 12-pdr cannons. General Braddock with his ADCs and staff with a guard "Foot & Horse", the main body of troops on each flank of the convoy of packhorses and cattle, a few gunners with a 12-pdr at the rear of the convoy and the rearguard. The long and narrow column also had small parties of troops detached as "Flank Guards" off to each side. They followed the trail moving west and entered a heavily wooded area.

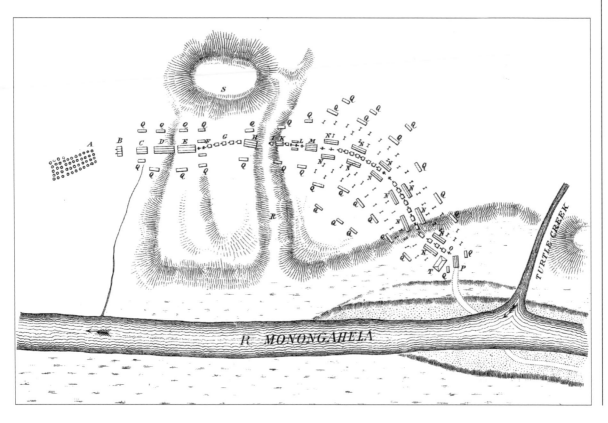

THE MONONGAHELA – THE AMBUSH

9 July 1755, viewed from the northeast showing the advance of General Braddock's column and the opening of the battle as Captain de Beaujeu's French, Canadians and Indians engage the head of the column.

Note: Gridlines are shown at intervals of ¹/₂ mile/0.8km

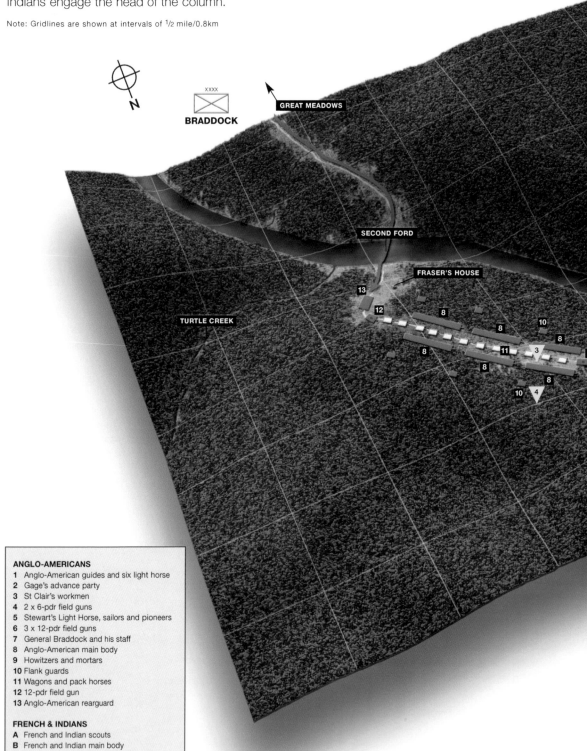

BRADDOCK

XXXX

GREAT MEADOWS

SECOND FORD

FRASER'S HOUSE

TURTLE CREEK

ANGLO-AMERICANS
1 Anglo-American guides and six light horse
2 Gage's advance party
3 St Clair's workmen
4 2 x 6-pdr field guns
5 Stewart's Light Horse, sailors and pioneers
6 3 x 12-pdr field guns
7 General Braddock and his staff
8 Anglo-American main body
9 Howitzers and mortars
10 Flank guards
11 Wagons and pack horses
12 12-pdr field gun
13 Anglo-American rearguard

FRENCH & INDIANS
A French and Indian scouts
B French and Indian main body

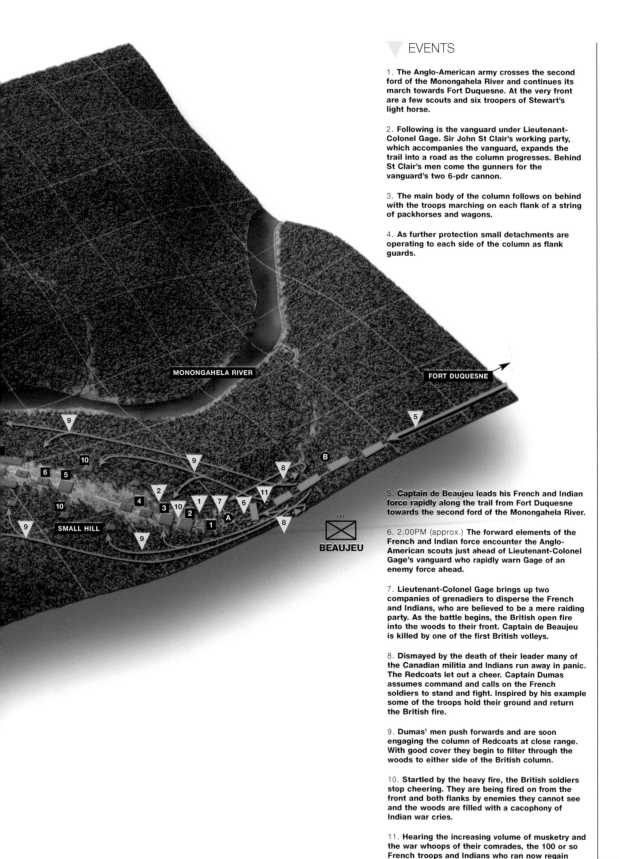

MONONGAHELA RIVER

FORT DUQUESNE

SMALL HILL

BEAUJEU

▼ EVENTS

1. **The Anglo-American army crosses the second ford of the Monongahela River and continues its march towards Fort Duquesne. At the very front are a few scouts and six troopers of Stewart's light horse.**

2. **Following is the vanguard under Lieutenant-Colonel Gage. Sir John St Clair's working party, which accompanies the vanguard, expands the trail into a road as the column progresses. Behind St Clair's men come the gunners for the vanguard's two 6-pdr cannon.**

3. **The main body of the column follows on behind with the troops marching on each flank of a string of packhorses and wagons.**

4. **As further protection small detachments are operating to each side of the column as flank guards.**

5. **Captain de Beaujeu leads his French and Indian force rapidly along the trail from Fort Duquesne towards the second ford of the Monongahela River.**

6. 2.00PM (approx.) **The forward elements of the French and Indian force encounter the Anglo-American scouts just ahead of Lieutenant-Colonel Gage's vanguard who rapidly warn Gage of an enemy force ahead.**

7. **Lieutenant-Colonel Gage brings up two companies of grenadiers to disperse the French and Indians, who are believed to be a mere raiding party. As the battle begins, the British open fire into the woods to their front. Captain de Beaujeu is killed by one of the first British volleys.**

8. **Dismayed by the death of their leader many of the Canadian militia and Indians run away in panic. The Redcoats let out a cheer. Captain Dumas assumes command and calls on the French soldiers to stand and fight. Inspired by his example some of the troops hold their ground and return the British fire.**

9. **Dumas' men push forwards and are soon engaging the column of Redcoats at close range. With good cover they begin to filter through the woods to either side of the British column.**

10. **Startled by the heavy fire, the British soldiers stop cheering. They are being fired on from the front and both flanks by enemies they cannot see and the woods are filled with a cacophony of Indian war cries.**

11. **Hearing the increasing volume of musketry and the war whoops of their comrades, the 100 or so French troops and Indians who ran now regain their composure and return to the field.**

63

It seems that de Beaujeu thought that Braddock's army might have been further away than it actually was. Like Braddock, he does not appear to have had scouts far ahead of his force probably hoping the many Indians with him would have scouts out already. Thus it was that neither force had precise knowledge of the exact whereabouts of the other. Commandant de Beaujeu's fast-moving force rapidly covered the seven miles, while the Anglo-American army was moving much more slowly from the ford, Lieutenant-Colonel Gage's vanguard having gone about three-quarters of a mile from Fraser's abandoned house.

At about 2.00pm, Gage's vanguard had just crossed a wide valley when its lead scouts and Virginia light horsemen, who were about 200 yards ahead, suddenly stopped, came back "and told [that] a Considerable Body of the Ennemy, Mostly Indians were at hand". Captain Gordon of the engineers was there plotting out the road; he rode up and thought that the "whole number" of French and Indians "did Not Exceed 300" and saw "an Officer at the head of them dressed as an

Indian, with his gorget on, waved his hat and they immediately dispersed to the right and left, forming a half-moon." The officer may have been de Beaujeu.

The opening clash

The two companies of British grenadiers accompanied by another 150 soldiers came up; Gage ordered them to fix bayonets and to form in order of battle. It was done "with the first rank [kneeling] upon the ground" and they opened fire into the woods in front of them. The volley's initial effect startled two cadets with the Canadian militiamen who started to panic; half of the militia, about 100 men, broke and ran yelling "sauve qui peut" (save yourselves if you can). French return fire was sporadic. The British brought up the two 6-pdrs, which also opened fire while the troops continued to fire volleys for a few minutes. On the third volley, Commandant de Beaujeu was killed. Seeing some of the Canadians and Indians flee, the British let out some cheers.[9]

At about 300 yards behind the vanguard was the main body under General Braddock. They could hear some shooting in front and the cheering of the soldiers up front. The troops in the main body made ready for action; it was probably just another of the hit-and-run skirmishes by a small band of French and Indians. There was every confidence that regulars in the vanguard would naturally soon prevail and scatter the mere "savages" ahead.

But all this confidence in the Anglo-American column was about to vanish. With de Beaujeu killed, command of the French and Indians devolved to Captain Dumas. The situation looked desperate and Dumas later wrote that, at that point, his only wish was to be killed rather than be defeated. Whatever his feelings, Captain Dumas was a brave man with

The grenadiers are shaken by the heavy fire. "Seeing no enemy, and themselves falling every moment from the fire" they stand their ground but some start to waver as officers encourage them. Print by Howard Pyle illustrating George Washington's account of the battle published in *Scribner's Magazine* in May 1893.

steady nerves in battle. He called on the French soldiers, Canadians and Indians who had not panicked to stand and fight with him. He then went forward with the courage "given by despair". His men were inspired by his example; many followed him and they soon came within close range of the column of redcoats. Finding good cover in the woods as they approached either side of the column, they opened a very heavy fire into the British ranks. The startled British soldiers stopped cheering. They could not see their enemies who had fanned out in the woods on both sides and now redoubled their shooting while shouting Indian war whoops.

The hundred or so Canadians and Indians who had started to flee, hearing the intense shooting and the war cries, recovered their nerve. They ran back to help their comrades and join in the action. Already many Indians and Canadians were ambushing the detached "Flank Guards" on each side of the column. Gordon later wrote that these flank parties "which only consisted of an officer and 20 men … were very soon Cut Off" from the main column. Confusion was growing in the British ranks as, suddenly, its flank guards were overwhelmed and the column fired on by a largely invisible enemy. In spite of the heavy odds against the French and Indians, the tactics of the "Canadian style of warfare" were starting to reap results.

At this point, Captain Dumas sensed things were starting to turn in his favor. He was with the French troops and Indians shooting at the front of the British vanguard. He now saw an opportunity to surround and engage the enemy at close range from cover and he seized it. By now, the Indians and Canadians with their regular officers and cadets were deployed in the woods on either side of the Anglo-American army. He sent orders to the officers leading Indians, such as de Langlade, to attack both sides of the Anglo-American column.

General Braddock had meanwhile sent an aide-de-camp, probably Captain Morris, to find out how things were going with the vanguard engaged in front. He expected they would have rapidly cleared the band of French and Indians they had run into; instead, shooting continued, and, indeed, grew more intense while horrific Indian war whoops seemed to echo everywhere in the dark forest all around. Quite suddenly things were not going according to plan. Hearing the "excessive quick and heavy firing in the front", General Braddock ordered more troops under Lieutenant-Colonel Burton to join the vanguard. This would add about 400 to 500 fresh soldiers to the engagement; there would soon be about 800 troops to deal with whatever was occurring at the front of the column. He sent out an order for Lieutenant-Colonel Burton's detachment to reinforce the vanguard and another to halt the march of the rest of the column. General Braddock now decided to immediately go to see for himself what was going on in front. Leaving Sir Peter Halket in command of the remaining 400 troops to safeguard the artillery and baggage in the rear, General Braddock then spurred his horse towards the action followed by Colonel Washington, Lieutenant Orme and the rest of his staff.

A desperate fight

Up front, the vanguard's line of grenadiers with the two 6-pdr cannons were firing into the woods in front of them, but to little effect as most of Captain Dumas' men had moved around to the flanks as the

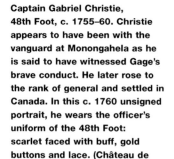

Captain Gabriel Christie, 48th Foot, c. 1755–60. Christie appears to have been with the vanguard at Monongahela as he is said to have witnessed Gage's brave conduct. He later rose to the rank of general and settled in Canada. In this c. 1760 unsigned portrait, he wears the officer's uniform of the 48th Foot: scarlet faced with buff, gold buttons and lace. (Château de Ramezay Museum, Montréal. Author's photo)

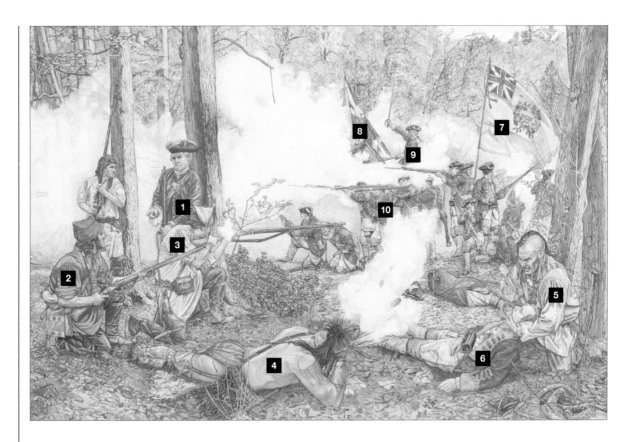

BRADDOCK'S DEFEAT AT THE MONONGAHELA, 9 JULY 1755
(pages 66–67)

In the initial clash with the Anglo-American vanguard, one of the first volleys killed Captain Beaujeu and some of the French and Indians panicked and fled. Captain Dumas and other officers subsequently rallied these men but rather than engaging the Anglo-Americans with conventional linear tactics, the French and Indians adopted the "Canadian" method of fighting. The French and Indians fanned out on both sides of the Anglo-American column and, from good cover within the forest, poured a heavy fire into the British column. British elation at their apparent initial success rapidly turned to confusion and dismay as this unseen enemy began to tear holes in the exposed ranks of the regulars. At left, a senior officer of the *Compagnies franches de la Marine* (1) reminds a Canadian militiaman (2) wearing a red cap to aim in particular for the British officers. These were particular targets for the French and Indians and heavy casualties amongst the officers added further to the confusion. In contrast to their British counterparts, the dress of French regular colonial troops officers on campaign in the wilderness demonstrated a great deal of variety. This officer wears his uniform laced hat and blue waistcoat laced with gold and his officer status is confirmed by the gilded gorget worn around his neck. Many officers, Captain Beaujeu included, adopted the Canadian style of dress on campaign, which was largely indistinguishable from Indian costume to the Anglo-Americans, although Beaujeu did retain his officer's hat. This Indian or Canadian style of dress has been adopted by one of the of the *Compagnies franches de la Marine* (3). An allied Indian (4) lying on the ground fires at the redcoats while to the right at the

edge of the forest an Indian chief (5) wearing a gorget is about to quickly scalp a fallen British soldier (6). This soldier is one of the many unfortunate men who formed the detached Flank Guards on each side of the column. He wears the regulation red coat with yellow facings of the 44th Foot. Due to the warm weather, the British infantrymen had changed from red cloth waistcoat and breeches to those made of 'Osnabrig' linen issued at the outset of the campaign. It was important, even in the heat of battle, for Indians to secure their trophy of a fallen enemy's scalp, a practice sometimes also adopted by Canadian and American woodsmen. In the background the men of the 44th Foot try to return fire on their elusive foe. During the battle, the British and American officers made increasingly desperate attempts to rally the confused and panicky soldiers to their regiment's colors. The silk regimental color shown (7) is in accordance with the Royal Warrant of 1747, the field being in the 44th's regimental facing color of yellow, its center is painted with "44" in Roman numerals surrounded by a wreath. In the canton was a small Union Jack. The King's color to the left (8) consisted of the Union Jack with regimental number in Roman numerals within a wreath at the centre of the cross of St George. A regimental field officer (9), a major or lieutenant-colonel as he is mounted, desperately tries to rally his men and deploy them in battle formation. He wears the somewhat plainer all-scarlet coat often used by officers in the field. The British infantry's standard practice of deploying in close-formed ranks (10) was utterly inappropriate for warfare in the wilderness and did little more than present their phantom-like enemies with a target it was virtually impossible to miss.
(Stephen Walsh).

Horatio Gates was a captain of a New York Independent Company at the battle of 9 July 1755 where he was wounded in the chest but was saved by Private Francis Penfold who managed to carry him off the field. He went on to become a general in the nascent American Army in 1775. In 1777, he achieved lasting fame when he accepted the surrender of General Burgoyne and his entire army at Saratoga. From a c. 1780 French print. (Anne S.K. Brown Military Collection, Brown University, Providence, USA. Author's photo)

engagement became general, and were now pouring their fire into the redcoats from both flanks. As grenadier after grenadier was hit and fell, the others wavered and then their line broke. Lieutenant-Colonel Gage saw he was outflanked and ordered a withdrawal so as to re-form about 30 yards behind. In doing so, Gage's men ran into the front of Lieutenant-Colonel Burton's command as they came up. Burton's men too were being fired upon and, as Orme related, he was forming his men "to face a rising ground to the right" from which "Indians" were firing down on his men. Burton's men were trying to form themselves into a firing line, according to Gordon, "in the greatest Confusion", and the arrival of Gage's men, some of them near panic, caused even more disarray. They were huddled "Altogether, the Advance & Main Body in Most places from 12 to 20 [men] Deep" forming superb targets for their foes who, safely under cover, took full advantage of this. The Anglo-American force now rapidly degenerated into "Confusion and Panic".

The officers tried to restore order and the colors of the 44th and 48th regiments "were advanced in different places, to separate the men of the two regiments", so as to form under their own officers. But their officers were falling even faster than the men and the rally to the colors failed. General Braddock was on the scene with his staff and, said Orme, "ordered the officers to endeavor to form the men, and to tell them off in small divisions and to advance with them; but neither entreaties or threats could prevail." The French and Indians were practically invisible, and now that a fog of musket smoke hung over the scene, even the flash and smoke from a hidden foe's musket had become indiscernible. A surviving British officer noted the result was that the Canadians' and Indians' "irregular method of fighting by running from one place to another obliged us [British soldiers] to wheel from right to left, to desert ye guns and then hastily to return & cover them." The American provincial troops added to the disarray, if possible, as they would "without any orders run up immediately some behind trees & others into ye ranks & put ye whole [British troops] in confusion."

In the meantime, Captain de Ligneris and other officers had followed Captain Dumas' orders to the letter. The initial panic had vaporized and the 900-man force was deployed along the full length of the Anglo-American column on both sides. The terrain, heavily wooded with numerous large trees, suited their tactics perfectly. "The Savages and Canadians kept on their Bellies in the bushes and behind the Trees, and took particular Aim at Our Men, and Officers especially", related Captain Stevens of the Virginia Rangers. They would normally not stay behind the same tree long but, having fired a shot, relocate behind another, load and fire, and so on. In this way, they could confuse the enemy as to their location and numbers. Consisting largely of Canadian militiamen and Indians, most of the force was armed with light-caliber Tulle hunting and trade muskets rather than the heavy-caliber military muskets. They were handling a very familiar weapon and were proficient at aimed fire rather than the volley fire prevalent in European armies. Indeed, chroniclers of the 18th century were unanimous in praising the skills of Canadians at target shooting with their light smoothbore muskets. This explains the vast numbers of Anglo-American casualties and also the high proportion of officer casualties, who were naturally prime targets. Their one potential weakness was the lack of bayonets, a disadvantage in hand-to-hand

THE MONONGAHELA – THE ROUT

9 July 1755, viewed from the northeast, showing the rapid disintegration of the Anglo-American force as their enemies swarm all round them in the woods, using their irregular tactics with devastating effectiveness.

Note: Gridlines are shown at intervals of $1/2$ mile/0.8km

ANGLO-AMERICANS
1 Gage's advance party
2 2 x 6-pdr field guns
3 Stewart's Light Horse, sailors and pioneers
4 3 x 12-pdr field guns
5 General Braddock and his staff
6 Anglo-American main body
7 Howitzers and mortars
8 Flank guards
9 Wagons and packhorses
10 12-pdr field gun
11 Anglo-American rearguard

FRENCH & INDIANS
A French and Indians

XXXX

BRADDOCK

GREAT MEADOWS

16

SECOND FORD

15

FRASER'S HOUSE

11

TURTLE CREEK

12

10 14

9

8

2

A

6

9

12

6

7

6

8

A

9

2

A

8

▼ EVENTS

1. **Captain Dumas senses that the situation is starting to turn in his favor. He is with the French troops and Indians engaged with the British vanguard at the front of the column. He now gives his officers orders for their men to fan out along each side of the column and engage the Redcoats at close range from behind cover.**

2. **With their regular officers and cadets now alongside them, the Indians and Canadian troops rapidly swarm down the flanks of the British column, all the while filling the woods with their intimidating war cries.**

3. **General Braddock orders the column to halt and then sends Lieutenant-Colonel Burton forwards with additional men to support the vanguard. This will put some 800 troops at the front of the column to deal with whatever is blocking the way.**

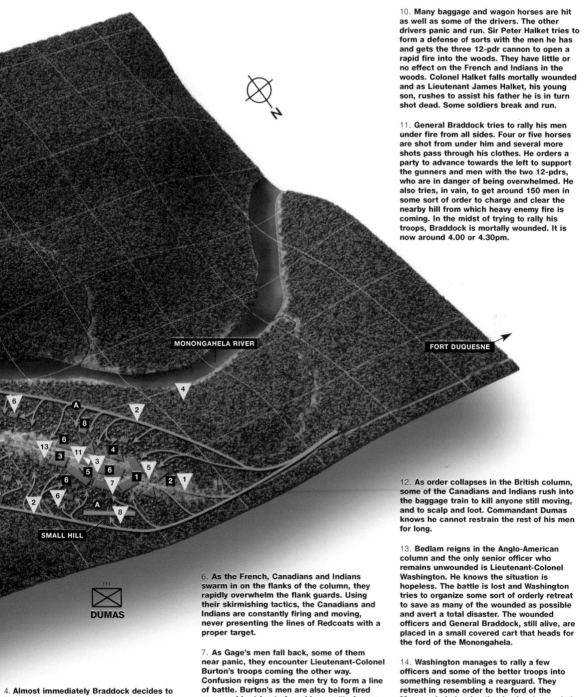

10. Many baggage and wagon horses are hit as well as some of the drivers. The other drivers panic and run. Sir Peter Halket tries to form a defense of sorts with the men he has and gets the three 12-pdr cannon to open a rapid fire into the woods. They have little or no effect on the French and Indians in the woods. Colonel Halket falls mortally wounded and as Lieutenant James Halket, his young son, rushes to assist his father he is in turn shot dead. Some soldiers break and run.

11. General Braddock tries to rally his men under fire from all sides. Four or five horses are shot from under him and several more shots pass through his clothes. He orders a party to advance towards the left to support the gunners and men with the two 12-pdrs, who are in danger of being overwhelmed. He also tries, in vain, to get around 150 men in some sort of order to charge and clear the nearby hill from which heavy enemy fire is coming. In the midst of trying to rally his troops, Braddock is mortally wounded. It is now around 4.00 or 4.30pm.

MONONGAHELA RIVER

FORT DUQUESNE

SMALL HILL

DUMAS

12. As order collapses in the British column, some of the Canadians and Indians rush into the baggage train to kill anyone still moving, and to scalp and loot. Commandant Dumas knows he cannot restrain the rest of his men for long.

13. Bedlam reigns in the Anglo-American column and the only senior officer who remains unwounded is Lieutenant-Colonel Washington. He knows the situation is hopeless. The battle is lost and Washington tries to organize some sort of orderly retreat to save as many of the wounded as possible and avert a total disaster. The wounded officers and General Braddock, still alive, are placed in a small covered cart that heads for the ford of the Monongahela.

14. Washington manages to rally a few officers and some of the better troops into something resembling a rearguard. They retreat in some order to the ford of the Monongahela leaving the dead and wounded, all the artillery and baggage on the battlefield.

15. At the ford, Washington deploys his improvised rearguard as effectively as circumstances allow, enabling many survivors to cross the river.

16. On the south bank of the river, Lieutenant-Colonel Burton, although wounded, tries to rally the soldiers and begs them to get into some order. Overwhelmed with panic, they will not stand and the remnants of Braddock's force stream away from the Monongahela as fast as possible.

6. As the French, Canadians and Indians swarm in on the flanks of the column, they rapidly overwhelm the flank guards. Using their skirmishing tactics, the Canadians and Indians are constantly firing and moving, never presenting the lines of Redcoats with a proper target.

7. As Gage's men fall back, some of them near panic, they encounter Lieutenant-Colonel Burton's troops coming the other way. Confusion reigns as the men try to form a line of battle. Burton's men are also being fired upon and he tries to form his men "to face a rising ground to the right" where "Indians" are shooting from. Gage's and Burton's men are soon huddled between 12 and 20 men deep. The Anglo-American force now degenerates rapidly into confusion and panic.

8. Practically invisible amongst the trees, the French, Canadians and Indians are presented with a target they cannot miss and aim in particular for the officers.

9. The French, Canadians and Indians move closer to the baggage and ammunition train, which they attack.

4. Almost immediately Braddock decides to inspect the situation at the head of the column for himself and moves forward with his staff, leaving Sir Peter Halket in command of the remaining 400 troops to safeguard the artillery and baggage in the rear.

5. The vanguard's grenadiers and the two 6-pdrs fire into the woods in front of them with little effect. Most of Captain Dumas' men are now on their flanks, pouring fire into the Redcoats from close range. With British soldiers falling all around, the vanguard begins to waver. Realizing he is outflanked, Lieutenant-Colonel Gage orders his men to withdraw and re-form some 30 yards to the rear.

combat with regular troops. The Canadians could withdraw very quickly, however, and were about to demonstrate that expert handling of the tomahawk more than compensated for the lack of a bayonet at close quarters. Already, they had overcome the weak flank guards, the survivors of whom had run into the confused center adding to the panic by shouting that the invisible enemy was on all sides.

Death and defeat

While General Braddock was trying to rally his men, the French and Indians at the rear moved closer to the baggage and ammunition train, which they "warmly attacked". Many horses were hit as well as some of the wagoners. The rest of the wagoners panicked and ran off. Sir Peter Halket tried to form a defense with the men he had and ordered the three 12-pdr cannon with the baggage train to open a rapid fire into the woods. Their ammunition was quickly being expended but the 12-pdrs had little or no effect on the scattered French and Indians in the woods. Colonel Halket was hit and fell mortally wounded, but the Halket family's tragedy did not end here. Sir Peter's youngest son, Lieutenant James Halket, rushed to his father's aid and was shot dead on the spot; some accounts say that he fell lifeless across his father's body.[10]

Under fire from all sides, General Braddock was himself a prime target for the Canadians and Indians and four or five horses were successively shot from under him and several more shots went through his clothes but he remained, so far, unscathed. The panic and confusion around him was supreme with the crazed soldiers crowded against each other loading and firing into the air as quickly as possible. He ordered a party to advance towards the left to support the gunners and men with the two 12-pdrs who were in danger of being overwhelmed. He also now knew that the two 6-pdrs with the vanguard had been left in the field and captured by the French who could turn them on their former owners.

The French, Canadians and Indians take positions on both sides of the column and, protected by trees and foliage, pour a heavy fire on the Anglo-American vanguard and main body. This late 19th century print gives a good sense of the action.

OPPOSITE **Sir Peter Halket, colonel of the 44th Foot, killed with one of his sons during the battle of the Monongahela on 9 July 1755. Print after Allan Ramsay.**

The troops escorting the wagons are also fired upon and soon in disarray. According to Lt Orme, "The advance flank parties, which were left for the security of the baggage, all but one ran in. The baggage was then warmly attacked; a great many horses, and some of the drivers were killed; the rest" of the teamsters ran off amidst a scene of utter confusion.

Each gun had by then fired between 20 and 30 rounds despite the gunners being prime targets for the Canadians and Indians. General Braddock ordered that the hill to the right be captured. He seems to have hoped to execute some sort of pincer attack by advancing one party to the left while seizing the hill on the right.

He tried in vain to get 150 men in some sort of order to clear the nearby hill, from which the enemy poured fire into the mass of redcoats. Colonel Washington had previously suggested attacking the hill with his Virginia provincials to "engage the enemy in their own way; but the propriety of this was not seen into until it was too late for execution", Washington wrote bitterly years later. By now two of General Braddock's three aides-de-camp, Morris and Orme, were wounded with only Washington left unscathed. General Braddock was reduced to rallying what men he could to try to attack the hill. Lieutenant-Colonel Burton at last managed to get together about 100 men of the 48th Foot and, Orme says, "prevailed upon them, by the General's order, to follow him towards the rising ground on the right, but he being disabled by his wounds, they faced about to the right, and returned." It was while Braddock was attempting to rally his troops that he was finally struck and fell with a mortal wound to the shoulder and the chest according to Washington, through his lungs according to Orme. It was around 4.00 or 4.30pm.

By now, all the senior officers had been hit: Gage, Burton, and St Clair were wounded, and now Braddock had suffered a grievous hurt. Scores of regimental officers lay dead or wounded along with hundreds of soldiers. The enemy's shooting was clearly quite accurate and the British soldiers' instinct to close ranks simply offered excellent targets even through the thick musket smoke. Many British soldiers were now seized by panic at the slaughter around them and ran, making their way as best as they could towards the Monongahela River. "They were infatuated to such a pitch," wrote Captain Steven, "that they would obey no Orders, killed one another & deserted the Colours."

The French soldiers, Canadian militiamen and Indian warriors were shooting as fast as they could, some starting to run low on ammunition. They were in excellent cover and all but invisible in the forest, concealed not only by the foliage but by the smoke. Thus, they had seen hardly any of their number fall while they could see British redcoats falling in droves. Captains Dumas, de Ligneris and other officers now had an increasing command and control problem with the Indians, and probably with many Canadian militiamen as well. They were eager to rush in to finish the job with tomahawk and scalping knife and get some booty. It was the only "pay" Canadian militiamen could expect, and, for the Indians, to get some prisoners to sell to French officers or to keep for their own purposes, ranging from adoption to a ghastly fate at the torture post. For Captain Dumas, the issue was obvious and he knew he had to let them charge in; the question was whether there might be a trap or reinforcements that might yet turn the tide. He and his officers had no way of knowing all the British commanders had been hit and that panic had set in among the Anglo-American troops, but they did not expect a relief force to be nearby.

Washington withdraws

Colonel Washington faced a hopeless situation. He was seemingly the only officer of rank that had not been killed or wounded. Four bullets had pierced his coat and two horses had been shot under him but he had escaped any injury. Around him, as he later wrote, "No person" knew the true extent of the army's disorder or "who the surviving senior officer was" so that "Troops by degrees were going off in confusion." The Anglo-American force was now in chaos and, Colonel Washington realized, could no longer fight and thus was "without a ray of hope left of further opposing [the enemy] from those [Anglo-American soldiers] that remained" in the field. The battle was lost. "The cannon silenced, & the Indian's shouts upon the Right Advancing, the whole Body [of British troops] gave way & crossed the Monongahela", Gordon recalled. It should be added that an officer's servant remembered the few Indians with General Braddock's army "behaved very well for the small quantity of them." But the rest of the army would not stand.

The issue was now to try to organize some sort of orderly retreat to save as many wounded as possible and prevent a total disaster. General Braddock was still alive and Colonel Washington "attended him on horse-back, tho' [he was] very weak and low." Braddock realized all "hope of rallying the dismayed Troops and recovering the ground [was] lost", he ordered Washington to retreat to Dunbar's camp. Colonel Washington then "placed the general in a small covered cart which carried some of his most essential equipage". This headed for the ford of the Monongahela River. According to Gordon, Orme and Morris, Braddock's wounded ADCs were also put into the cart.

Some sort of rearguard had to be organized and Colonel Washington managed to rally some officers and men of "the best troops" who were still being fired upon, and retreated in some order to the ford of the Monongahela leaving the dead and wounded, all the artillery and

Lieutenant Robert Orme, ADC to General Braddock, was wounded in the action. He was an officer in the Coldstream Guards and so is usually referred to as "Captain Orme", which is correct as a Guards' commission was equivalent to the next senior rank in the line infantry (and also more expensive). Orme survived the ordeal and wrote one of the best journals of the campaign. Print after Sir Joshua Reynolds.

A largely invisible enemy in the surrounding forest fires on the British regulars and American provincial troops from all sides. Many men fall around General Braddock who is also hit, with Colonel Washington at his side. Officers on foot nearby try to reach the general to support him. Print after H.A. Ogden.

baggage on the battlefield. Near the ford, Colonel Washington's improvised rearguard was "formed in the best order circumstances would admit on a piece of rising ground." Thus many survivors crossed the river. Lieutenant-Colonel Burton, although wounded, tried to rally the soldiers and "made a speech to the men to beg them to get into some order" but they were overwhelmed with panic. In the end, everyone hurried off from the Monongahela River as fast as possible.

The French & Indians descend on the battlefield

At the site of the action, the shooting subsided while the Indian war whoops had redoubled. Seeing what was left of the enemy column on the run and hundreds of bodies strewn around, the excited Indians, Canadian militiamen and French soldiers had left their covered positions and descended in a rush, yelling Indian cries and scalped and finished off all they could. The "pillage was horrible", reported Captain Dumas who now had lost all control of his force. The majority were allied Indian nations, not a regular military force, who could not be controlled and this was their reward and glory. A good many Canadian militiamen, especially those enlisted for such wilderness expeditions, were equally fierce warriors, having spent part of their lives amongst the Indians as minor traders and canoe men. Even some French regulars, long stationed by choice in such forts as Michilimackinac, had adopted wilderness ways.

General Braddock falls mortally wounded from his horse having being hit at the height of the battle of the Monongahela while utter confusion reigns around him. A late-19th century print after P. Philippoteaux.

Meanwhile, the wounded French officers were left without assistance in the nearby woods when all had descended on the field. Captain Dumas ordered Lieutenant Le Borgne and another officer to the field to call on some soldiers busy looting to help their wounded officers. To their credit, Dumas reported, the soldiers came to their senses and all rallied to this task and they carried them to Fort Duquesne. although two officers died of their wounds on the way. Having now too few soldiers left to carry the body of Commandant de Beaujeu, he was lain hidden in a small ravine for the time being. Meanwhile, on a field given over to indiscriminate looting to the sound of war whoops, the *Compagnies franche de la Marine* sergeants kept their cool and immediately seized the British powder kegs, which they spread on the ground before some crazed looter got to them. These were near the British guns, which they then dismantled as best they could to render them unusable. No one had nails to plug the cannons' vents. Captain Dumas sent a courier to Commandant de Contrecoeur at Fort Duquesne to send him some but he only got them the following day.

Flushed with such an extraordinary victory, Captain Dumas was also dismayed at the sudden disintegration of his own force. He only had a handful of regular officers and men left. The Canadian militiamen were out of control, although they would come back in due course. As for the Indians, they had done their part and most were already on the way back to Fort Duquesne with their prizes and prisoners. They were seen arriving at the fort by James Smith, a Pennsylvania road worker previously captured by Indians, with "a great many bloody scalps, grenadiers' caps, British canteens, bayonets, &c, with them" constantly firing off their muskets answered by the fort's cannons "which were accompanied by the most hideous shouts and yells from all quarters." Some unfortunate prisoners "stripped naked, with their hands tied behind their back, and their faces and part of their bodies blackened" were also brought into the Indian camp near the fort and put "to death on the banks of the Allegheny River opposite the fort" often screaming "in a most doleful manner" at the touch of red-hot irons. It was one of the terrifying customs of North American Indians to put prisoners to

The mortally wounded General Braddock is placed "in a small covered cart" by Colonel Washington according to his account of the battle. The event was illustrated by Howard Pyle and published in the May 1893 issue of *Scribner's Magazine*.

WASHINGTON'S REARGUARD, 9 JULY 1755 (pages 78–79)
By late afternoon the "battle" of the Monongahela had degenerated into a slaughter. General Braddock had received a mortal wound, although he still lived, and scores of regimental officers had been killed or wounded along with hundreds of the rank and file. The Anglo-American column had collapsed into chaos as cohesion disintegrated and increasing numbers of men refused to obey orders and fled. As Captain Stephen wrote, "They were infatuated to such a pitch that they would obey no Orders, killed one another & deserted the Colours." Colonel Washington (1) was the only senior officer that had not been killed or wounded. That he remained unscathed seemed almost miraculous considering the fate of the other officers and that he had two horses shot under him and four bullets passed through his coat. He realized that the force around him was collapsing before his eyes and no longer capable of sustaining the fight. Although one officer's servant commented that the few Indians with Braddock's army, "Behaved very well for the small quantity of them", the rest of the army would not stand. The battle was lost. The best Washington could hope for now was to extract as many of the surviving troops and wounded as possible, and possibly save the baggage. Braddock himself was placed in a small covered cart, along with his wounded aides-de-camp. If anything was to be saved from the wreck, some form of

rearguard must be organized. Colonel Washington managed to rally some of "the best troops" and retreat in some order towards the Monongahela. His force most probably contained a high proportion of the surviving grenadiers (2), but doubtless also included men from the battalion companies (3) and a scattering of the more resilient Virginia militiamen (4). The wounded and the baggage had to be abandoned and the footsteps of Washington's men were dogged every step of the way by the French and Indians (5). As he neared the ford of the Monongahela, which the men had crossed that morning with such confidence, Washington's rearguard "formed in the best order circumstances would admit on a piece of rising ground" (6). These men were the exception, however, and most fled for their lives in panic (7), some dragging wounded comrades with them (8) rather than abandon them. In this way a number of survivors safely crossed the river that would otherwise probably have fallen to the muskets, knives or tomahawks of their pursuing foes. This could only provide a temporary respite and the pressure from the French and Indians finally overwhelmed Washington's men and they too fled. Across the Monongahela, Lieutenant-Colonel Burton, although himself wounded, tried desperately to rally the fugitives but, overwhelmed with panic, they hurried off south in the direction of Dunbar's camp as fast as possible. (Stephen Walsh)

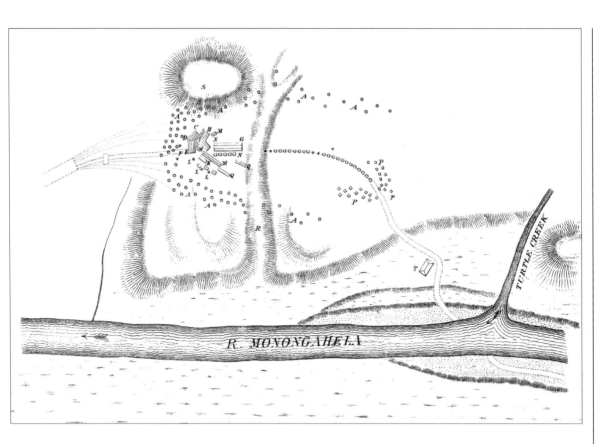

Disposition of the troops towards
the end of the action on 9 July
1755 according to Engineer
Patrick Mackellar. A, the French
and Indians behind trees; C, D,
E, H, K, M, N and Q, the British
and Americans in disorder; F and
L, field pieces; P, rear guard.

death by ritual torture. Condemnable practices in the eyes of Europeans
whose societies practiced unspeakable tortures on prisoners in the name
of justice or religion.[11]

The rest of the Indians had found liquor in the abandoned baggage,
probably the issue army rum, and stayed on the battlefield to get utterly
drunk. Amidst all this carnage, Captain Dumas was concerned about
a British counterattack. Lieutenant Desligniéres reported to Captain
Dumas that the French force hardly had anyone left and that the British
still had "about 800 fresh men" nearby. Whether this force was confused
with the troops that colonels Washington and Burton had tried to rally
or with Colonel Dunbar's column is not clear. After council with his
officers, Captain Dumas ordered a withdrawal to about a mile from the
action so as to regroup "our little army which had suffered few losses and
was only dispersed" so as to be ready should the Anglo-Americans
advance again the next day.

On 10 July, Captain Dumas greeted "the Indians who had spent the
night drinking on the battlefield" who were coming back "with a few
officers who had stayed with them". These would have been officers
operating with the Indians such as Ensign de Langlade. They reported
that the British were marching towards them and that they had heard
drums beating. Captain Dumas knew that he was in fact without any real
intelligence as to enemy movements and did not give much credence to
such reports by hung-over Indians smelling of rum. He went back to the
battlefield with a hundred soldiers and Canadian militiamen to recover
the British artillery left there. He also sent a messenger to Fort Duquesne
for dugout canoes to meet him. Commandant de Contrecoeur imme-

diately sent Ensign de Céléron up the Monongahela River from the fort with 12 dugout canoes manned by six men each. They paddled to the area of the battlefield. There, the cannons were most likely put into the canoes at the ford and then sent back to Fort Duquesne. Smith recalled seeing "Braddock's artillery brought into the fort; the same day I also saw several Indians in British officers' dress, with sash, half moon [gorgets], laced hats, &c." Back on the battlefield site, Captain Dumas and his men were being told "by every Indian that came to us, that the enemy was coming" but Dumas did not believe it; he had sent out two scouting parties, most likely Canadian militiamen, and they came back to report that the Anglo-Americans were nowhere nearby.

For Captain Dumas, a pursuit was impossible. Besides his officers, he had perhaps ten soldiers left with him. The Canadian militiaman would not be very enthusiastic at such a move without their many Indian friends and these had now vanished with their booty. Although later criticized for not pursuing, Captain Dumas was undoubtedly right when he told his critics that the force left to him could not have prevailed; even if he had wanted to "push his luck", he did not have the means to do it. Thus, after being assured that the Anglo-Americans were soundly beaten and would not be back, Captain Dumas and his men returned to Fort Duquesne. The Ohio Valley remained within the realm of King Louis XV of France and as far as ever from British control.

Rear view of a British Army tumbrel cart. It was in such a cart that the mortally wounded General Braddock was carried away from the field of Monongahela. Reproduction at Fort Ligonier. (Author's photo)

Retreat to Dunbar's camp

Far from plotting a counterattack, the Anglo-Americans were in a complete rout. Attempts by some officers to rally the men had no success at all, "nothing would do" and indeed, there was fear that, if pressed, the soldiers would "desert us", related a wounded Lieutenant Gordon of the engineers. Therefore, the officers "were obliged" to go along with their men and everyone was obviously in a hurry. The survivors of Braddock's army were in such fear of Indian pursuers that they "never halted" and marched all night on the road they had built a few days earlier. George Washington recalled this night march as horrific with "the dying, the groans, lamentations, and crys along the road of the wounded for help … were enough to pierce a heart of adamant. The gloom and horror of which was not a little increased by the impervious darkness occasioned by the close shade of thick woods." At dawn the next day, 10 July, the survivors were still on the move and as apprehensive as ever; although increasingly tired, they marched all day until about 10.00pm when they came to Gist's abandoned settlement. There they decided to stop, no doubt totally exhausted. They had marched for about 30 hours without a break and covered an incredible 60 miles (97km) or so from the field of battle. Gist had, incidentally, survived the ordeal and was probably rather pleased to see his old place again, even in ruins. The men slept there, no doubt posting guards, as they remained nervous of lurking French and Indians.

Colonel Dunbar was made aware of the disaster by a terrified wagoner who galloped into his camp with the news at five in the morning on 10 July. Another arrived to confirm the story and, at one in the afternoon, a wounded Sir John St Clair "who saw the whole" battle rode in giving a more complete account. There seemed little point in mustering a force to advance, but rather to prepare for the hundreds of survivors approaching his camp. As Gist's settlement was only six miles away, the remnants of the army started reaching Dunbar's camp on 11 July, including that evening the wagon bearing the mortally wounded General Braddock. It was now obvious that the remnants of the army including Dunbar's force would have to return to Fort Cumberland. As the senior surviving and unwounded officer, Dunbar was now in command of the army. On 12 July, therefore, he ordered provisions and ammunition destroyed, while "great Numbers of Wounded Officers and Soldiers Arrived." On 13 July, the army moved out abandoning Dunbar's camp and marched towards Fort Cumberland.

This journey marked the last few hours of General Braddock's life. As the retreating army neared Great Meadows on 13 July, he passed away at eight in the evening. His ADC, Colonel Washington, saw to it that he "was interred with the honors of war". The spot where he was buried was then hidden with wagons passing over it "to hide every trace by which the entombment could be discovered" lest it should be found and desecrated by the French and Indians. A monument now marks the spot where what are believed to be his remains were found. It is near Fort Necessity and Jumonville Glen.

The battered army did not remain at Great Meadows for long. A return of the different companies showed that, excluding officers, some 896 non commissioned officers and private soldiers were lost. The grenadiers had suffered the most: 70 of 79 from Dunbar's 48th Foot were lost, 57 of 70 from Halket's 44th Foot recorded one of the surviving sailors. The sailors for their part had 18 killed or wounded out of 33. The army now marched in a regular fashion with vanguard, rearguard and piquets. The women and servants were to stay with the provost at the rear on pain of "severe punishment". The next days were difficult for the wounded, all those who could march being ordered to do so assisted by escorts.

At last, on 17 July, the army reached Fort Cumberland. The wounded were taken care of, the musket balls removed and their wounds dressed. The campaign to capture Fort Duquesne and secure the Ohio Valley had ended in a resounding defeat.

Horrendous casualties

The count of dead and wounded on the British and American side was horrendous. Participants usually estimated about 1,000 casualties out of some 1,200 or 1,300 souls in the column, including at least 450 killed. The leading officers had been killed or wounded including the commanding general. All the artillery and baggage had been lost. It ranked as one of the worst disasters in the annals of the British Army.

The French casualties were trifling by comparison although they included the death of Captain de Beaujeu. Also killed in action were Lieutenant de Carqueville, Ensign de La Pérade, two regular soldiers, three Canadian militiamen and 15 allied Indians. The grand total came to 23 killed including the 15 Indians. A lieutenant, an ensign, two cadets,

Monument at the site where General Braddock is believed to have been buried after the battle. It is only about a mile from Fort Necessity. (Author's photo)

two regular soldiers, two Canadian militiamen and 12 Indians were wounded for a total of 20. French and Indian casualties thus came to 43 including 27 Indians.

Amongst the items found by the French on the battlefield were General Braddock's papers including his instructions from King George II and those from the commander-in-chief, the Duke of Cumberland, as well as copies of letters from the duke to several ministers such as the Duke of Newcastle, Secretary at War Henry Fox, Secretary of State Sir Thomas Robinson and the Earl of Halifax. These were real prizes and were sent from Fort Duquesne to Québec. There, Governor General Vaudreuil saw their political importance and had "very true copies" made and sent them on to the Count Maurepas, the Minister of the Navy at Versailles. Once translated, the papers were useful to French diplomats pressing their cases insofar as the rights of France and the aggressive usurpations they accused the British of plotting. The French government published them in 1756.

4   According to J.C.B. the French then received "a volley of musketry which the enemy aimed at them; at this time, the Sieur de Jumonville, as his duty called, had the summons which he carried read; the enemy paid no attention to it and a second volley killed Sieur de Jumonville and nine of his men. The others, to the number of 24, were taken prisoner and brought to Winchester." J.C.B. also states he got his account from Monceau and from allied Indians who came in two days later, giving more details on who had been killed, wounded and made prisoner. It was confirmed by "an English prisoner that arrived a few days later." He described Monceau as "a man of 36 years of age, robust, very agile at running, speaking several Indian languages as he had always been on friendly terms with them and had been to war and hunting with them since his youth."

5   Ensign Drouillon was not a Canadian but a French metropolitan officer who had arrived in Canada in 1752. Following his request to become familiar with the frontier, he had been sent to the Ohio with Captain Marin in 1753 and participated in the construction of forts Presqu'Isle, Le Bœuf and Duquesne. After his capture he was sent to England and released to France in 1755. He came back to Canada, was promoted to lieutenant in 1757, present at the battle of Ste Foy in 1760 and repatriated to France later that year.

6   Yet another version of the encounter is a family tradition of the de Villiers family. Jumonville was the great-uncle of Philippe Aubert de Gaspé who wrote in the 1860s that the "tradition in my family is that Jumonville was the bearer of a summons … that he hoisted his flag of truce and showed his dispatches, but that nevertheless the English commandant ordered his men to fire on him and his little escort, and that Jumonville fell mortally wounded, as well as those who accompanied him" as per Philippe Aubert de Gaspé, *Les Anciens Canadiens* (Québec, 1863 and many reprints). Some of this must have been later hearsay as he has Jumonville reading the summons at Fort Necessity. In Québec, the Sieur de Courville stated basically the same version (except for Fort Necessity) in his *Mémoire sur le Canada* (Québec, 1838) written in the 1750s and 1760s.

7   According to J.C.B., the Indians had also captured six more retreating Anglo-Americans who were taken directly to Fort Duquesne. Commandant de Contrecoeur wanted them to be released but, after having had these prisoners run the gauntlet, the Indians gave back two and kept four as hostages.

8   De Contrecoeur's dispatch to Governor General Vaudreuil dated 21 June 1755 is especially informative as to actions taken by the French to gather information on the progress of General Braddock's army. It is difficult to read being written in a rather phonetic style but it is clear enough that parties were constantly sent out to observe and, if possible, harass. The parties would be mostly Indians with officers and cadets. There may have been more reports like this but if so, they appear to have been lost. *Papiers Contrecoeur*, pp.364–366.

9   The cheer was "vive le roi" (God Save the King) according to Captain Dumas' account.

10 Some years later, in about November 1758 following the fall of Fort Duquesne, the celebrated artist Benjamin West and Captain (but local rank of Major) Francis Halket, 44th Foot, Sir Peter's other son, went to the battlefield to search for remains. "They found two skeletons — one lying across the other — Halket looked at the skulls, and said faintly 'It is my father'" as per Thomas Carter, *Historical Record of the Forty-Fourth of East Essex Regiment* (Chatham, 1887), pp.11–12.

11 The French had little choice but to tolerate the Indians' customs towards prisoners although roundly condemned by the British who, on their side, were equally tolerant of such practices by their own Indian allies such as the Iroquois. The French authorities attempted with varying degrees of success to humanize the treatment of prisoners brought back from expeditions by attempting to free the latter from their Indian allies, especially through purchase. Numerous accounts by people taken prisoner in New England contain dreadful descriptions of the tortures endured, but point out as well the efforts made by officers in New France to obtain their release. A different fate awaited French and Canadian prisoners. Colonies such as Massachusetts paid handsome bounties to their Indians for enemy scalps with no barriers on age: the scalps of children were worth £19 and children taken prisoner were sold back for £20. In addition, the scalps of children over 12 years of age were worth £38 and the prisoners themselves £40. This very slight difference between the value of scalps and prisoners amounted to a veiled invitation to kill those captured rather than take the trouble to take them in. Thus, there are no accounts of French or Canadian prisoners as they were obviously murdered.

AFTERMATH

Colonel Dunbar fell back all the way to Philadelphia setting up his "winter quarters" there despite it being only August! This led Lieutenant-Governor Dinwiddie to comment that he appeared "to have determined to leave our frontiers as defenseless as possible." With the British regulars decimated and disorganized, the colonies of Virginia and Maryland did what they could to beef up frontier defenses and raise some troops. Little could be expected from the pacifist Quakers ruling Pennsylvania. In Virginia, Lieutenant-Governor Dinwiddie ordered out the militia, but found it to be cowardly and "seized with panick". Three companies of rangers (also called "independent companies") were quickly raised. Fort Cumberland was to be immediately reinforced with another 50 men from Virginia as this fort now became the first line of defense, there being no Anglo-American presence west of it. Other measures were in hand. On 14 August 1755, George Washington was commissioned colonel of a new Virginia Regiment of 1,000 men as well as being appointed commander-in-chief of all Virginia forces. The regiment already had some 800 men in its ranks in September. Unlike most provincial units in more secure places, the Virginia Regiment was kept on service with some 500 men on duty during the winter of 1755–56. Following General Braddock's defeat, the Maryland legislature authorized 80 men to serve on the frontier for four months. A more substantial measure by Maryland was the building of Fort Frederick, a large bastioned stone walled structure east of Fort Cumberland. Should Fort Cumberland fall to the French and Indians, Fort Frederick would be a powerful deterrent to any enemy moving east towards the settled areas of Maryland and Virginia.

In Fort Duquesne, Captain Dumas succeeded a sickly de Contrecoeur as commandant by order of Governor General Vaudreuil in August. By then the vast majority of the Indians that had taken part in the battle had returned home, however much French officers tried to keep them at Fort Duquesne. Some did stay or came back and others joined after a few weeks. As there were few regulars and Canadians in the Ohio, the Indians were essential to hold the Americans at bay. With the situation so favorable following the crushing of General Braddock's army, Commandant Dumas did all he could to encourage Indians to mount raids, and for many months to come the frontier of the American colonies came under increased Indian attack. This was a terrifying turn of events for the American frontier settlers, and many of them evacuated their dwellings. Raids from Fort Duquesne reached almost as far as the coast and even into South Carolina.

Elsewhere in North America, the French were not as fortunate as they had been in the Ohio. In Nova Scotia, Lieutenant-Colonel Robert Monkton led a force of some 2,000 regulars and provincials that captured forts Beauséjour and Gaspareau on 16 June 1755 after a brief

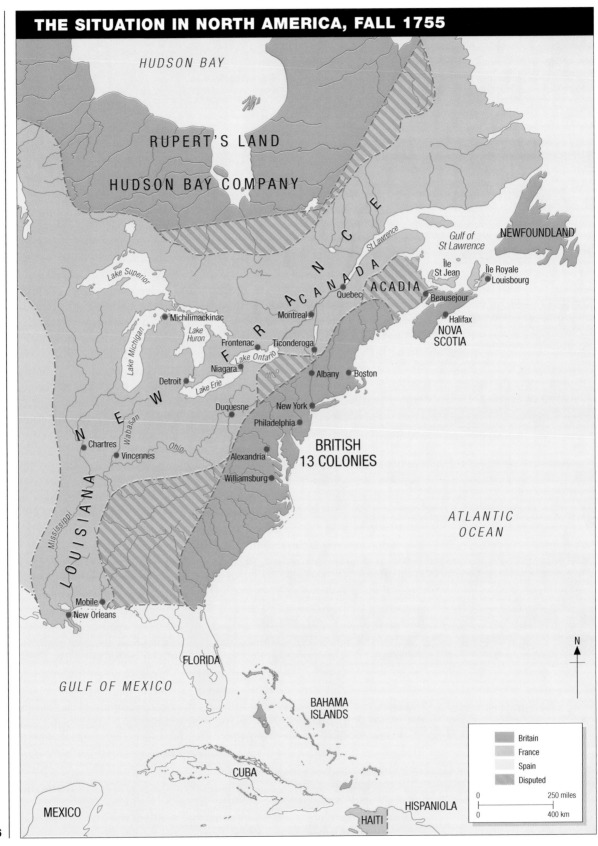

HUDSON BAY

RUPERT'S LAND

HUDSON BAY COMPANY

NEWFOUNDLAND

Gulf of
St Lawrence

Lake Superior

St Lawrence

F R A N C E

Île
St Jean

Île Royale
Louisbourg

C A N A D A

A C A D I A

Quebec

Beausejour

Montreal

Halifax

NOVA
SCOTIA

Michilimackinac

Lake
Huron

Lake Michigan

Frontenac

Ticonderoga

Niagara

Lake Ontario

Detroit

Lake Erie

Albany

Boston

N E W

Duquesne

New York

Wabasan

Ohio

Philadelphia

Chartres

BRITISH
13 COLONIES

Vincennes

Alexandria

Williamsburg

L O U I S I A N A

Mississippi

ATLANTIC
OCEAN

Mobile
New Orleans

FLORIDA

GULF OF MEXICO

N

BAHAMA
ISLANDS

MEXICO

CUBA

HISPANIOLA

HAITI

	Britain
	France
	Spain
	Disputed

0   250 miles

0   400 km

Fort Frederick, Maryland, was built after General Braddock's defeat to block sizable French expeditions penetrating further east into the heart of the state. A large bastioned fort with stone walls, it served as a base for later Anglo-American expeditions. It has been restored and is now an historic site. (Author's photo)

siege. This cleared the way for the deportation of the hapless Acadians, one of the most tragic events in Canadian history, which later inspired Henry Wadsworth Longfellow's celebrated poem: *Evangeline*. On the Lake Champlain/Lake George front, the French built a powerful fort at Ticonderoga and, in September, General Dieskau advanced to attack some 3,000 American provincial troops led by Colonel William Johnson in an entrenched camp at the lower end of Lake George. Dieskau commanded some 1,500 troops, including the 2nd battalions of the regular army *La Reine* and *Languedoc* regiments sent over from France. In spite of the advice of allied Indians, Canadian regular officers and militiamen, General Dieskau insisted on a frontal, European-style attack on 8 September. The assault failed and General Dieskau was wounded and captured by the Americans. It was a fiasco for the French, although casualties were not as heavy or the strategic significance as great as the events of 9 July on the banks of the Monongahela River.

The two sides drew different lessons from the battles of Fort Necessity and Monongahela. The French, as victors, saw little to improve upon in terms of woodland warfare tactics and Indian diplomacy. Despite this extraordinary triumph, metropolitan tacticians in France continued, as in the past, to ignore tactical doctrine championed by the Canadian officers. The Marquis de Montcalm, who replaced Dieskau, would clash with Governor General Vaudreuil on that subject as well as many others. Senior French officers and military theoreticians, while wanting to emulate Prussian and Austrian light troops and tactics, never grasped the significance of their own "home grown" tactics developed in Canada.

By contrast the sheer scale of the disaster made the British and Americans seriously reassess the way the campaign had been waged. Lord Loudoun was appointed to replace the fallen General Braddock and, as one of Britain's finer strategists, he was sympathetic to tactical innovation if it could secure success. He listened to what British and American officers, such as Gage and Washington, had to say and encouraged the formation of rangers and light troops. More significantly he felt this should not be limited to American frontiersmen but should also be practiced by selected British regular soldiers grouped in light units. The

Earl of Loudoun was succeeded by General Abercromby who, after his disastrous frontal attack on Ticonderoga in July 1758, was in turn replaced by Sir Jeffrey Amherst as commander of the forces in North America. Amherst, who had just captured Fortress Louisbourg, used light troops in conjunction with his line battalions and proceeded cautiously, not wishing to replicate the fates of Braddock and Abercromby.

A renewed attempt to win the Ohio Valley was made again in 1758, with a mixed British and American army of about 7,000 men under the command of Major-General John Forbes marching on Fort Duquesne. The lessons of Monongahela were such that, despite having three times as many men as General Braddock, General Forbes was extremely patient and methodical, systematically building a road with supporting forts across the wilderness. He nevertheless suffered difficulties of his own, notably when the French crushed his vanguard of 800 men under Major James Grant in September, and the near-disastrous French raids on Fort Ligonier in the following months. Ultimately, Forbes' road had reached within a few miles of Fort Duquesne when, on 26 November, its French garrison blew it up as they retreated. By early 1759, the British flag finally flew over the Ohio Valley.

Their victory over an army of British Redcoats also reinforced Indian confidence in their irregular tactics. When they next faced a regular army in 1763, however, the French and Canadians were not alongside them. British commanders and troops had by then become much more adept at light infantry tactics and Chief Pontiac's Indians were beaten at Bushy Run, Pennsylvania, not far from the battle site of Monongahela. Colonel Henri Bouquet, who commanded the British troops at Bushy Run, was himself a disciple of light infantry tactics.

Ultimately, in the final third of the 18th century, the French developed their light infantry in line with experience acquired in Europe, while the British, and eventually the Americans, adapted theirs as a result of their experiences on campaign amid the North American wilderness.

ORDERS OF BATTLE

Ambush of Jumonville, 27 May 1754

French
Ensign de Jumonville, Officer Commanding
Compagnies franches de la Marine – 2 officers (including Jumonville), 3 cadets, 1 drummer, 1 interpreter, 26 soldiers and Canadian militiamen
Total: 33

Anglo-Americans
Lieutenant-Colonel George Washington, Officer Commanding
Virginia provincial troops – about 40
Indians – 30 (approx.)
Total: 70–80 (approximately)

Casualties
French: 10 killed including Ensign de Jumonville, 1 wounded, 21 taken prisoner (only one Canadian militiaman named Monceau escaped)

Anglo-Americans: 1 killed

Fort Necessity, 3 July 1754

French
Captain Louis Coulon de Villiers, Officer Commanding
Compagnies franches de la Marine and Canadian militiamen – about 500 men
Indians – at least 100, possibly as many as 300

Anglo-Americans
Lieutenant-Colonel George Washington, Officer Commanding
Captain McKay's South Carolina Independent Company – 100
Virginia Provincial Regiment – about 300

Casualties
French: 2 killed, 17 wounded
Indians: 1 killed, 2 wounded

Anglo-Americans: 31 killed, 70 wounded

General Braddock's Army, June 1755[12]

Major-General Edward Braddock, Officer Commanding

Royal Artillery, Capt Ord's Company – 60
Royal Navy sailors – 33
Indians – 8 (approx.)
Capt Robert Stewart's Virginia Provincial Troop of Horse Rangers – 3 officers, 34 troopers, 8 batmen.

First Brigade – Colonel Sir Peter Halket
Halket's 44th Foot – 700
Captain Rutherford's New York Independent Company – 95
Captain Polson's Virginia Provincial Artificers (or Carpenters) – 3 officers and 48 enlisted men.
Captain Peronnee's Virginia Provincial Rangers – 3 officers and 47 enlisted men.
Captain Wagner's Virginia Provincial Rangers – 3 officers and 45 enlisted men.
Captain Dagworthy's Maryland Provincial Rangers – 3 officers and 49 enlisted men.

Second Brigade – Colonel Thomas Dunbar
Dunbar's 48th Foot – 650
Captain Demeries' South Carolina Independent Companies detachments – 97
Captain Dobb's North Carolina Provincial Rangers – 3 officers and 80 enlisted men.

Captain Mercer's Virginia Provincial Artificers (or Carpenters) – 3 officers and 35 enlisted men.
Captain Steven's Virginia Provincial Rangers – 3 officers and 48 enlisted men.
Captain Hogg's Virginia Provincial Rangers – 3 officers and 40 enlisted men.
Captain Cox's Virginia Provincial Rangers – 3 officers and 43 enlisted men.

Total: about 2,150 officers and men

Battle of the Monongahela, 9 July 1755

French
Capt de Beaujeu, Officer Commanding[13]
Compagnies franches de la Marine – 13 officers, 36 cadets, 72 NCOs and privates, (total 121)
Canadian Militia – 146
Indians – 637
Total: 904

Anglo-Americans[14]
Major-General Edward Braddock, Officer Commanding
Aides-de-Camp: Lieutenant Robert Orme, Coldstream Guards; Captain Roger Morris, 48th Foot; and Lieutenant-Colonel George Washington, Virginia Provincials
Secretary: William Shirley
Deputy Quartermaster General: Sir John St Clair
Assistant Deputy Quartermaster General: Lieutenant Matthew Leslie, 44th Foot
Major of Brigade: Lieutenant Francis Halket, 44th Foot

Royal Artillery – 20
Royal Navy sailors – 33
Indians – 8 (approx.)
Captain Stewart's Virginia Provincial Troop of Horse Rangers – 29
Halket's 44th Foot – 450
Dunbar's 48th Foot – 450
Captain Rutherford's New York Independent Company – 50
Captain Peronnee's Virginia Provincial Rangers – 50
Captain Wagner's Virginia Provincial Rangers – 50
Captain Steven's Virginia Provincial Rangers – 50
Captain Polson's Virginia Provincial Artificers (or Carpenters) – 50

Total: 1,200 to 1,470 officers and men (approx.).

Casualties:

French and Indians:
Capt de Beaujeu, Officer Commanding – killed

Compagnies franches de la Marine – Killed: 2 officers, 2 privates. Wounded: 2 officers, 2 cadets, 2 privates.

Canadian Militia – Killed 3. Wounded 2.
Indians – Killed 15. Wounded 12.

Total French and Indian casualties: 43 (killed 23, wounded 20).

Anglo-Americans
Major-General Edward Braddock, Officer Commanding – killed
Secretary: William Shirley – killed
Staff officers – 2 wounded
Engineer officers – 3 wounded

89

Officers
Halket's 44th Foot – 6 killed, 8 wounded
Dunbar's 48th Foot – 6 killed, 12 wounded
Royal Artillery – 1 killed, 2 wounded
Capt Rutherford's New York Independent Company – 1 killed, 3 wounded
Volunteers – 2 wounded
Royal Navy – 2 killed
Captain Robert Stewart's Virginia Provincial Troop of Horse Rangers –1 killed,
    1 wounded
Virginia companies – 5 killed, 2 wounded

Royal Navy midshipmen – 1 killed, 1 wounded
Chaplain – 1 wounded
Quartermaster – 1 wounded
Surgeon's mates – 1 killed, 5 wounded
Sergeants – 17 killed, 20 wounded
Drummers – 2 killed, 6 wounded
Privates and matrosses – 386 killed, 328 wounded "many of whom were afterward
    killed by the Indians"
Royal Navy mates and sailors – 10 killed, 8 wounded

Notes:
The above is based on Alexander Hamilton's letter to his brother in August 1755
but there are many variances in contemporary accounts. The total of British regular
and American provincial NCOs and privates killed and wounded has been
compiled as high as 914 out of 1,373; the total of officers killed and wounded is
given as 63 out of 86 making a grand total of some 1,000 killed, wounded and
missing. The figure also does not include batmen, officers' servants, wagoners and
women.

    According to Engineer Mackellar, the Anglo-American army engaged in the field
came to 1,469 including 96 officers. Out of these, he reported that 456 were killed
including 26 officers, 520 were wounded including 36 officers, for a total of 976
killed and wounded.

State of the Artillery … found on the battlefield[15]
Four brass cannons with the cipher of England, of five and a half pounds caliber.
Four [idem] of eleven pounds at sixteen ounces a pound.
Four brass howitzers with the arms [ciphers] as idem of seven and a half pounds
    of diameter.
Three brass mortars with the cipher of England of four inches and thirteen lines.
(…) The six cannons and howitzers are spiked.

---

12 These are approximate numbers as of June 1755.
13 Killed in action and replaced by Captain Dumas.
14 These are approximate numbers based on musters before and after the
    battle reproduced in Sargent and Pargellis.
15 Dated at Québec, 8 August 1755, in Pargellis, *Military Affairs* …, p.131.
    Another report dated 3 August mentioned six 6-pdrs instead of four. This
    would include guns abandoned at Little Meadows. Archives Nationales
    (France), Dépôt des fortifications des colonies, file for Canada.

THE BATTLEFIELDS TODAY

In 1754–55, the three battlefields of Jumonville Glen, Fort Necessity and the Monongahela were an unsettled wilderness crossed here and there by narrow Indian trails situated in what is now the western part of the state of Pennsylvania. Today one can easily drive to all three sites: from the east, Interstate 68 heads west through the state of Maryland. A stop to visit Fort Frederick, which is remarkably well preserved and restored, is strongly recommended. Cumberland, Maryland, is the site of Fort Cumberland at Will's Creek, and the fort's site has been preserved as a park with a small cabin used by George Washington. Leave I-68 at Keysers Ridge and take Highway 40 west into Pennsylvania. Just past the village of Farmington are the sites of Fort Necessity and Jumonville Glen, both National Historic Battlefields administered by the US National Park Service.

Jumonville Glen is probably the site that has remained least changed from 1754. Having parked your vehicle, a walk through narrow forest trails leads to the top of the cliff where Washington and the Half-King's men observed Jumonville's party below. A number of good interpretation panels help to understand the situation in 1754. At the foot of the cliff is the flat area where the action occurred. The author's impression, after visiting this site twice, is that it was the ideal place for an ambush and that the French party certainly saw itself on a diplomatic mission to deliver an ultimatum and did not expect to be attacked. As the Virginians

The somewhat sprawling and derelict US Steel plant at Braddock, Pennsylvania, occupies part of the battle site. (Author's photo)

considered Jumonville's party to be a French war band, this was an ideal place for an attack.

Nearby, on Highway 40, is Fort Necessity National Battlefield. Set in a large clearing partly surrounded by forest, it is indeed a "Great Meadow" having a small circular stockade fort with some earthworks outside at one end. The fort was rebuilt on the site following archeological excavations done in 1952–53, and must have been an incredibly cramped place for some 400 men. The interpretation center is nearby. It is a very pleasant area to walk around and see the various features of the battlefield, which are well-marked. A walk up the wooded hill just north of the fort gives a sense of how the French and Indians perceived the place. It was not a bad site and such a fort could have held its own against a sizable raiding party but did not stand a chance against de Villiers' large force of at least 600.

The site of the battle of the Monongahela, covered by forest in 1755, mostly cleared with fields by 1855, was totally built over with heavy industry in what became the town of Braddock in the later 19th and early 20th centuries. For a time, it was a booming town with a very large steel mill and its many related industries, which totally transformed the area. The once wild Monongahela River itself was rerouted as a canal for the iron ore barges and its flow regulated by low dams. Such a dam with locks was built just about where Braddock's army crossed the second ford. On the south shore is now the Kennywood Amusement Park with its large Ferris wheel. This is on the spot where Lieutenant-Colonel Burton and some of the officers vainly tried to rally the fleeing soldiers in the late afternoon of 9 July. Across the river is the large US Steel Mon Plant and its auxiliary industries which appear to have been built over much of the battlefield. Further west is the center of the town of Braddock, once a thriving place but now very much run down with decrepit buildings and mills, something of a post-industrial casualty. Finding features of the battlefield is a challenge in such an environment of urban decay, especially as even some of the topography appears to have been leveled when the industries were built. Certainly, it bears no resemblance to the natural site described in battle reports.

Heading west for a further eight miles (12.8km) or so brings one to the very center of the city of Pittsburgh at the meeting of the Monongahela and the Allegheny rivers where they form the Ohio River. At the meeting point is a superb park with a fountain and a round plaque marking the center of Fort Duquesne. The fort's walls are outlined on the ground. Slightly further back is the outline of the larger British Fort Pitt, built after Fort Duquesne was blown up, which has a museum in a rebuilt bastion. The center of Pittsburgh itself is a modern and most pleasant place with lots of restaurants and stores and small parks, a delight to stroll in. Driving north from Pittsburgh on I-79 will bring one to Erie with its noteworthy Maritime Museum and monument at the site of Fort Presqu'Isle. A drive down highway 19 leads into the small town of Waterford, the site of Fort Le Bœuf, which has a small museum as well as a park with a statue of George Washington handing out Governor Dinwiddie's summons in December 1753.

BIBLIOGRAPHICAL SOURCES

The British and American archival record concerning these events has very largely been published. Nevertheless, anyone venturing into the Public Record Office's Colonial Office class 5 (America and West Indies) volumes for the years 1754–55 will not regret it. France's "Archives Nationales" hold records mostly in series B, C11A and F3 of its "Colonies" series at the "Archives d'Outremer" depot in Aix-en-Provence. The National Archives of Canada in Ottawa and the Library of Congress in Washington hold further original records as well as transcripts and microfilms of records in European archives and libraries.

The French published records of these events are fewer and usually in French. Possibly the most valuable compilation is Fernand Grenier, ed., *Papiers Contrecoeur* (Québec, 1952), which forms an essential source of published documents. Louis Coulon de Villiers' journal relating the Fort Necessity campaign was sent to France and a shortened edited version was published in the *Mémoire contenant le Précis des faits ...* (Paris, 1756). Fernand Grenier's *Papiers Contrecoeur* publishes an original complete copy preserved at the archives of the Québec Seminary. Another original of this document is in Archives Nationales (France), Colonies, series F3, Vol. 14. Francis-J. Audet's *Jean-Daniel Dumas: le héros de la Monongahéla* (Montréal, 1920) reproduces Dumas' account of the battle. Another valuable account is by J.C.B., *Voyage au Canada fait depuis l'an 1751 jusqu'en l'an 1761* (Québec, 1887) and despite its author, the gunner Joseph Charles Bonin, mixing up some dates and events, as it was written many years after the events, it relates details found nowhere else but must be used with caution.

The published records of these events in English start with R.A. Brock, ed., *The Official Records of Robert Dinwiddie* (Richmond, 1883); its two volumes have scores of important letters. Winthrop Sargent, ed., *The History of an Expedition Against Fort Duquesne in 1755* (Philadelphia, 1856) remains an essential study with many published documents, notably Orme's journal. Andrew J. Whal, compiler of *Braddock Road Chronicles 1755* (Bowie, 1999) publishes extracts of numerous original sources in chronological order making this work another essential compilation. Stanley Pargellis, ed., *Military Affairs in North America 1748–1765* (New York, 1936) also reproduces key documents and maps pertaining to the 1755 battle.

There are numerous studies of the events of 1754–55. The attractive booklet by Martin J. West, ed., *War for Empire in Western Pennsylvania* (Fort Ligonier, 1993) provides a good summary. The various forts are well documented and illustrated in Charles M. Stotz, *Outposts of the War for Empire* (Pittsburgh, 1985). Paul E. Kopperman, *Braddock at the Monongahela* (Pittsburgh, 1977) is a detailed account, and Lee McCardell, *Ill-starred General: Braddock of the Coldstream Guards* (Pittsburgh, 1958) a biography of the ill-fated general. Volumes 3 and 4 of the *Dictionary of Canadian Biography* (Toronto, 1974–1980) include biographies of many of the participants.